ARNOLD BENNETT
Romantic Realist

By the same author

The Shaping of *The Dynasts:* A Study in Thomas Hardy (1967)
The Madness of Art: A Study of Henry James (1962)
Art and Substance in George Meredith (1953)
Romance and Tragedy in Joseph Conrad (1949)
Sensibility in English Prose Fiction: 1760–1814 (1937)

ARNOLD BENNETT

Romantic Realist

Walter F. Wright

UNIVERSITY OF NEBRASKA PRESS · LINCOLN

Publishers on the Plains
UNP

Copyright © 1971 by the University of Nebraska Press

All rights reserved

Library of Congress Catalog Card Number 75-144393
International Standard Book Number 0-8032-0798-0

Manufactured in the United States of America

To Huong and Suong

Contents

Acknowledgment

I wish to express my appreciation to Mr. N. Emery of the Stoke-on-Trent Libraries and to Mr. A. Mountford, Head of Museums at Stoke, who made available materials by and concerning Arnold Bennett; to Professor L. T. Hergenhan of the University of Queensland for reading the manuscript; and to Mrs. Dorothy Cheston Bennett for copyright permissions. To A. B. W. I am indebted as always.

Introduction

IN THE ATTEMPT to define patterns in literary history it is
natural to attach labels to authors to fit them neatly into
a scheme. The difficulty, of course, is that, although
minor, imitative writers can be assigned convenient
pigeonholes, the major ones range far too widely, both in
their appreciations and in their artistic methods. And yet,
in speaking of important Victorian and early twentieth-
century novelists one may make very good use of the
familiar pair of contrasting terms—romantic and realistic.

Of the many definitions of romance and realism perhaps
the most useful in the consideration of Victorian and
Edwardian novelists is Henry James's in his preface to *The
American*. Contrasting the "real" and the "romantic,"
James writes:

> The real represents to my perception the things we
> cannot possibly *not* know, sooner or later, in one way or
> another . . . . The romantic stands, on the other hand, for
> the things that, with all the facilities in the world, all the
> wealth and all the courage and all the wit and all the
> adventure we never *can* directly know; the things that
> can reach us only through the beautiful circuit and
> subterfuge of our thought and our desire.

James notes that a writer is of greatest interest "when he commits himself in both directions; not quite at the same time or to the same effect, of course, but by some need of performing his whole possible revolution, by the law of some rich passion in him for extremes."

Part of what makes Arnold Bennett especially interesting is that throughout his life he found himself attracted in both directions. At the very beginning he chose as artist to cultivate realism—more specifically its technique—but he soon recognized in himself a strong romantic bent. So it was that in his works we discover again and again his "rich passion . . . for extremes."

Doubtless all generations are in one way or another transitional, but for novelists the years from the 1890's on into the twentieth century seem to have been unusually so. The early and mid-Victorian novelists were still popular, but new subject matter and new techniques, influenced by the French and Russians, were being tried. It was in a changing literary milieu that Bennett flourished —restive with what had been achieved by earlier British novelists, mildly experimental in his own writing, and, as a critic, sometimes hesitant, sometimes daringly receptive toward things that were new.

ARNOLD BENNETT
Romantic Realist

CHAPTER ONE

The Savor of Existence

IN LATE JANUARY, 1906, the weather was mainly fine in Paris. Arnold Bennett was busy with articles and a light "fantasia," *The Sinews of War*. Though working hard, as always, he managed to dine with friends and to take leisurely strolls in the neighborhood of the Métro, the Concorde, and the Place de l'Opéra. As he walked he was both an author gleaning hints and a man from Burslem for whom Paris continued to wear a thin veil of mystery and glamor. In his *Journal* for January 29 he recorded his enjoyment of the "crowded pavements, little curiosity shops, and the continual interest of women"; and he concluded his entry, "I have had several days of regular unhurried work lately, interspersed with such strolls. I have come to the conclusion that this is as near a regular happiness as I am ever likely to get." [1]

The tone is far from ecstatic, for life was rarely for Bennett an unalloyed delight. There were always the complexities, the reservations, the need to be cautious, the anxieties, often vexatious and oppressive. Instead, the lines have a touch of wistfulness, the frank, unsophisticated

[1] All references, by date only, are to *The Journal of Arnold Bennett*, ed. Newman Flower (New York: The Viking Press, 1933).

wistfulness that never deserted the noted author and man of the world despite his urbanity and *savoir-faire*. They are echoed both early and late in the *Journal*, beginning in 1896 and concluding more than three decades later. In fact, the *Journal* and the "pocket philosophies" abound in references to the "miraculous interestingness of the universe." [2] Sometimes, as in letters to close friends and in his light fiction Bennett could, indeed, indulge in the pursuit of good-natured fun.

But the fragility of even so reserved an enjoyment as he found that twenty-ninth of January is revealed in very different comments which, though infrequent, persist in intruding into the *Journal*. On a summer day twenty-eight months later Bennett should have had reason for contentment, for he ended his record of May 26, 1908, with the fact that on re-reading Part I of *The Old Wives' Tale* he found it "devilish good." Still, he was disturbed. Earlier in the day he had tried as he repeatedly did to make the conscious mind prevail over circumstance: "I had been preaching to myself that it was my Reason's business to manufacture my happiness out of the raw material of no matter what environment I found myself in." But his dissatisfaction with the conditions of his life and with his own temperament led to a simple, undisguised admission of desolation:

> As at meals I sat between E., in tears and full of disasters, and Mme. Bergeret, an old woman, untidy, *radoteuse*, *maniaque*, though witty sometimes, and M. [Marguerite] away in Paris, the unpleasant, empty, unsatisfying greyness of existence weighed on me. I *en voulait* against E. for being unfortunate, and against Mme. B. for being old and *maniaque*, and I wanted to be surrounded by youth, beauty, and worldly success.

[2] *Literary Taste: How to Form It* (New York: George H. Doran, n.d.), p. 12.

The conscious mind could not prevent recurrence of similar moods down through the years. Thus it was that some nineteen years later, December 28, 1927, Bennett reviewed a particularly distressing winter evening. Mrs. Bennett having gone to the theater, he tried desultory reading and listening to the radio, and in his boredom he even spent an hour at the *Cinderella* pantomime, but nothing would do, and the *Journal* entry concludes, "This is the third successive evening that I have spent alone. I can stand almost anything better than a solitary evening. I can't tolerate many more." It is his wish, on the one hand, to find life miraculously interesting and, on the other, his inescapable awareness that it could be lonely and empty that give the savor to Bennett's own life and to his fiction.

Work itself was in part an escape from ennui and loneliness. As early as 1903, in *The Truth about an Author*, Bennett wrote, "Like most writers I was frequently the victim of an illogical, indefensible and causeless melancholy; but one kind of melancholy could always be explained, and that was the melancholy of idleness."[3] The mind must be occupied, if only in turning out popular articles or concocting ingenious stories of suspense. When it was not hurried along to turn out copy or grapple with mundane affairs, it would feel the oppression of circumstance. Bennett could create and for a while live in an imaginary realm, but he could not escape from his temperament. Sometimes the restiveness was purely mental, but there are many passages in the *Journal* and the fiction which dwell upon the physical sensation of discomfort. Bennett did not have to imitate the French naturalists in this; he gravitated toward the depressing and only by an effort drew back.

[3] *The Truth about an Author* (Westminster: Archibald Constable & Co., 1903), p. 216.

Bennett's descriptions of the Five Towns include eloquent praise of their picturesqueness beneath the canopy
of smoke; but many others stress the chill, the bleakness,
the sense of desolation. In London, too, Bennett was often
depressed by the affronts to his senses. There are hints in
his nonfiction that support the several references in the
novels to the cheerlessness of club rooms and restaurants.
In *A Man from the North* (1898), which admittedly drew
upon the author's own sensations, he once sums up his
hero's feelings: ". . . the meanness of the room, of his
clothes, of his supper, nauseated him."[4] Yet Bennett
seemed drawn toward dreary, dingy restaurants almost as
much as toward the opulent ones because there was more
of interest there. They were indeed depressing—and also
absorbing.

The *Journal* reveals his frequent restlessness because his
own apartment or house was uncongenial, and the novels
have much on the darkness, the cold, the oppressive emptiness of houses. The living quarters and the shop of the
Baineses in *The Old Wives' Tale* are seldom really pleasant.
More often one feels the chill and the want of sunlight. In
Hilda Lessways the drawing room of Hilda's mother is
"death-cold." In fact, chill and barrenness characterize
many rooms in the Five-Towns novels, especially the
Clayhanger trilogy. The boarding house which Hilda
manages at Brighton is not only tasteless, but depressing,
and to Hilda all Brighton is "a colossal and disgusting
enlargement of her own kitchen."[5] That Hilda is personally discouraged is irrelevant, for the evidence before
her eyes and all around her has been largely responsible
for her gloom, and she feels it with her whole being.

To philosophize about mutability is to treat it as some
abstract concept, perhaps without sensing its reality. For

---

[4] *A Man from the North* (New York: George H. Doran, 1911), p. 38.
[5] *Hilda Lessways* (New York: George H. Doran, 1911), p. 530.

Bennett it was not to be rendered harmless by reason. He felt decay and death as tangible entities, and, when not present, they were always lurking near. The pathetic decline of his father as he weakened both physically and mentally remained one of Bennett's strongest impressions, and in his *Journal* November 20, 1914, he dwelt on the cruelty of his mother's last hours: "Her condition was very distressing (though less so than the Pater's), and it seemed strange that this should necessarily be the end of a life, that a life couldn't end more easily." Interestingly, in the entry for November 24, having recorded her death, he went on to speak of the room in which he had that day been entertained at tea: "Cold upstairs room, with bedroom grate . . . . Three great windows. I got near the morsel of fire."

Bennett's preoccupation with his own health displays a mixture of vexation and melancholy. Most of the scores of references to insomnia and biliousness or headache end with a lament for his resulting inability to work, but others suggest a haunting anxiety, a noting of symptoms of irrevocable decay. When he cried out in anguish he was speaking of the temporary annoyance. He had the good taste not to burst out in unrestrained self-pity concerning his own mortality. Instead, in the *Journal* he drew from the lives of others evidence of the loss of vigor and hope and above all of beauty, the playthings of age, and he returned to the themes repeatedly in the pocket philosophies and the fiction.

Typical are *Journal* notes of May 31 and June 2, 1904. In the second Bennett gives an ironic portrait of a shabby, dirty old painter who is trying unsuccessfully to copy the antithesis of himself, a Raphael head in the Louvre. The man seems "absolutely disgusted, hopeless, and feebly bitter"; and Bennett comments, "I could not help feeling shocked by the sight, for of course this man had started out in life with the idea that he was going to succeed as a painter." Two days earlier he had witnessed what should have been a delightful scene. Two brothers and two sisters had been making merry on an outing and Bennett spoke of them as "so human, and so French, and so naïve." Then came his reflection: ". . . and the fleeting charm of the girls (neither of them pretty) was so soon to fade, and the men were so soon to become mature and *bête*." To be sure, Maupassant had expressed sentiments very like these, and perhaps a sentimentalist writing self-consciously for someone looking over his shoulder could have said much the same. But in the *Journal* there is always the ring of freshness and sincerity; in the best sense of the word the *Journal* is indeed naïve. The sisters were profoundly significant for Bennett, and he found their cousins again and again—in Italy and Greece, along the North Sea, and in London and Burslem; and their fictitious counterparts, which already included Leonora, were to reappear in the daughters of John Baines, in Hilda Lessways, and in a number of other women and girls who linger but briefly within the pages of his books.

Age and death were the touchstones. What then could one do in their ever-encroaching shadows? For Bennett there was the consolation of philosophy, but by itself it was far from enough. One might try to contemplate eternal verities, but he lived in a complicated social universe, in which he was no mere appreciative consciousness, but a self-conscious individual responsible for his own acts and susceptible to very personal rewards and rebuffs. Hence came his great need for success, a success to be measured not only by a feeling of artistic achievement, but by the external trappings which society uses to stamp its endorsement.

Usually Bennett's self-congratulations are oblique, but now and then he came forth with an unashamed avowal.

In "The Novel-Reading Public" (1909), at a time when his impressive list of titles included *The Old Wives' Tale*, he remarked with asperity that he had been born "slightly beneath" the middle class. The next sentence is naïve and also significant: "But by the help of God and strict attention to business I have gained the right of entrance into it."[6] Bennett continued with an attack, almost a tirade, on the middle class for its cultural deficiencies, and there was no humbug in his denunciation. It is nonetheless revealing that he felt he had earned the right to damn without being accused of envy. Twenty years later, despite his popularity as an author, he was still somewhat ill at ease and defensive. The enemy was epitomized in the Bloomsbury group, and most notably in Virginia Woolf. The precise nature of the quarrel will concern us later. At the moment what matters is the implication that Bennett was an inferior writer, catering to common minds. In a review of *A Room of One's Own*, in 1929, he disclaimed any feud, and yet he could not resist the gratuitous animadversion, "True, she is the queen of the high-brows; and I am a low-brow. But it takes all sorts of brows to make a world . . . ."[7] Actually, of course, Bennett's finest work was by no means low-brow. But he was disturbed by the recognition given to his merely popular books, particularly the fantasias, and by self-disparagement he tried to exclude his purely journalistic hack writing from consideration. Typical is a remark in the *Journal* for May 30, 1919: "I hope to finish my damnable, pedestrian, fair-minded, sagacious woman book on Monday."

Bennett was always sensitive to the difference between the pronunciation he had learned in Burslem and that which for him typified sophistication—the "lah-di-dah"

[6] *The Author's Craft and Other Critical Writings of Arnold Bennett*, ed. Samuel Hynes (Lincoln: University of Nebraska Press, 1968), p. 76.
[7] *Ibid.*, p. 225.

of South Kensington. According to J. B. Atkins he insisted that the best English was spoken "in the midlands."[8] In *The Old Wives' Tale* (1908), and again in *These Twain*, eight years later, he goes slightly out of the way to bring up the issue, and in each instance he mildly satirizes his own penchant. Thus Miss Chetwynd speaks "with a southern refinement which the Five Towns, while making fun of it, envied."[9] When Clayhanger is suddenly brought among persons from the south he fights the battle anew. He finds charm in the easy manners of Devonshire society, but is scornful of their "lah-di-dah" accent,

> which falsifying every vowel sound in the language, and several consonants, magically created around them an aura of utter superiority to the rest of the world. He quite unreasonably hated them, and he also envied them, because this accent was their native tongue, and because their clothes were not cut like his, and because they were entirely at their ease.[10]

Bennett was aware that success, of whatever kind, whether social or personal, was meted out to him in incomplete fragments. In reading the *Journal* one is impressed with the great range of experience, but also with its notelike fragmentation. It is not that Bennett should have sentimentalized incidents by trite philosophizing. On the contrary, the simple statement of his immediate sensations is refreshing. But there emerges an impression of a vast welter and a sense that Bennett himself was bewildered by life's magnitude and multiplicity. The tone is often one of malaise. The reading in George Moore and the French naturalists may have accentuated Bennett's feeling, but the preoccupation with frustration

---

[8] J. B. Atkins, *Incidents and Reflections* (London: Christophers, 1947), p. 176.

[9] *The Old Wives' Tale* (New York: George H. Doran, 1911), p. 63.

[10] *These Twain* (London: Methuen and Co., 1962), pp. 295–296.

and with his loneliness in a world where things often confronted him as a succession of separate, unrelated entities was there from the first.

One of Bennett's aphorisms may be indicative. "The best is good enough for me" sounds like a harmless bit of bravado. It was invented, however, by a man who was especially conscious of the drab, the boring, and the depressing. Enjoyment of luxury hotels, either actual or fictitious, and of yachts, and prominence in the world of letters, and ability to secure high prices even for casual articles were all very well; but uncertainty about the nature of the universe and his own place in it could sometimes bring an ache which resembled the spirit of the *fin de siècle*, yet was very personal to the "man from the North" who, in London, Paris, and elsewhere, was trying to find his identity.

In his search Bennett derived only limited help from the philosophers. Though his *Journal* is crowded with the names of novels in which he had at least browsed, and though he considered himself unusually well informed in music and painting, he reveals amazingly little systematic, historical knowledge of philosophy. For example, though May 23, 1908, he says that he "continued reading Lewes's *History of Philosophy*," which he had begun three days before, there is no further reference to it in the *Journal*. Three names make up his primary list—Marcus Aurelius, Epictetus, and Herbert Spencer: and he did not study any of the three as systematic philosophers. Indeed, his interest in Spencer was mainly in his sociological and scientific theories. In the *Journal* December 11, 1903, he agreed with Wells that Spencer was a "woolly" thinker. In *Sacred and Profane Love* (1905) reprinted as *The Book of Carlotta*, the heroine praises the *Introduction to the Study of Sociology* for teaching "how to think honestly." [11] September

[11] *The Book of Carlotta* (New York: George H. Doran, 1911), p. 13.

25, 1907, Bennett notes in the *Journal* that Spencer's *Genesis of Science* is a "superb example of his power of building a solid superstructure on the basis of a single axiom." In *How to Live on Twenty-Four Hours a Day* (1908), he casually alludes to Spencer as "the greatest mind that ever lived," [12] and a few pages later he praises *First Principles*. December 17, 1909, he records having read *The Study of Sociology* "all week." In *Literary Taste*, of the same year, he again tosses in praise of Spencer. In none of these numerous allusions, however, mainly from 1907 to 1909, is there evidence of careful pursuit of Spencer's ideas. The only indicative comment is on his method of reasoning.

Epictetus and Marcus Aurelius were intriguing to Bennett because of their stress on mental discipline. August 6, 1907, he writes in his *Journal* that in interpreting the Stoics to his friend Frederick Marriott he probably failed to make clear "what I meant by control of the mind and its consequences," and that earlier in the day he was unsuccessful in trying to put Stoic teachings "into practice in my relations with Mme. L." There are several allusions to both philosophers in the *Journal* for 1907–1908. September 16, 1907, Bennett, suffering from insomnia, remarks that not even they could "ensure cheerfulness and perfect equanimity." March 28, 1908, he writes confidently, "No mistake, the constant practice of M. Aurelius and Epictetus has had its gradual effect on me." April 3, he lectures himself on the importance of living for today, and he adds, "Sheer M. Aurelius of course." In *How to Live* he continues to cite the two Stoics; and in *The Human Machine* (1909), he sums up, "Not much has been discovered since their time." [13]

[12] *How to Live on Twenty-Four Hours a Day* (New York: George H. Doran, 1910), p. 39.

[13] *The Human Machine* (New York: George H. Doran, 1909), p. 98. The pocket philosophies appeared first as journalistic articles. To George Sturt, Bennett wrote, November 4, 1907, that much of his printed work for 1907

In *Clayhanger*, of 1910, however, Bennett's hero, tired and dejected, feels that his diligent study of both has been futile: ". . . he was enthusiastic to others, about the merit of these two daily philosophers; but what had they done for him? Assuredly they had not enabled him to keep the one treasure of the world—zest." [14] Clayhanger's thoughts sound like Bennett's own personal confession. Again, in 1922, in *Mr. Prohack*, there is an oblique admission that the teaching of Marcus Aurelius may not avail. The tone in which Bennett describes Prohack's predicament is playful, but the verdict is distinct:

> It was designed to fit the case of Mr. Prohack, for its message was to the effect that happiness and content are commodities which can be manufactured only in the mind . . . . But he would not have it. He said to himself: 'This book is all very fine, immortal, supreme, and so on. Only it simply isn't true. Human nature won't work the way the book says it ought to work; and what's more, the author was obviously afraid of life, he was never really alive and he was never happy. Finally the tendency of the book is mischievously anti-social.' [15]

In *The Book of Carlotta* Bennett quotes from *The Imitation of Christ* on the need for humility. In "My Religion," a short, undated article, he stresses the moral value of Christ's teaching and suggests that he got from *Anna Karenina* years before the notion that the main argument for God is man's conscience. As for the nature of God and His purposes, he laconically remarks, "Why should I agitate myself over a matter which exceeds my mental

was "nothing but Marcus Aurelius & Christ assimilated & executed by me in suitable form" (*Letters of Arnold Bennett*, Vol. II, *1889–1915*, ed. James Hepburn [London: Oxford University Press, 1968], p. 220).

[14] *Clayhanger* (London: Methuen and Co., 1962), p. 530.

[15] *Mr. Prohack* (Birmingham: C. Combridge, 1962), pp. 256–257.

powers?"[16] In his *Journal 1929* Bennett speaks of having read the Bible at some length, and he makes the obvious comment that it is "full of mysticism."[17] A line from the forty-sixth psalm—"Be still, and know that I am God"—is interestingly the favorite biblical phrase of the neurasthenic young Gracie of *The Imperial Palace* (1930). The line somehow reminds the hero of "Saul, smitten on the way to Damascus."[18] All these allusions are casual; they certainly lack the profound emotion with which Thomas Hardy, for example, read the Book of Psalms, Ecclesiastes, and the Book of Job. It would appear that Bennett did not find much in the tragic character sketches and the poetic depiction of religious awe that could supply either intellectual structure or comfort to a man of the nineteenth and twentieth centuries.

The very few comments on other works of a philosophic or religious nature are equally casual and disconnected. March 30, 1908, Bennett writes of having unsuccessfully devoted two days to a résumé of Bergson. His *Journal* note concludes: "Not the first time I have failed to interest myself in metaphysics. History and general philosophy much more in my line." For "general" one could read "practical." The same year, in *The Human Machine*, he recommends Annie Besant's *Thought Power* and implies familiarity with her other theosophistic works, as well.[19] In *Self and Self-Management* (1918), he boldly labels F. H. Giddings a brilliant social philosopher. In *Things That*

---

[16] Bennett *et al.*, *My Religion* (London: Hutchinson and Co., n.d.), p. 9.

[17] *Journal 1929* (London: Cassell and Co., 1930), p. 164.

[18] *The Imperial Palace* (New York: Doubleday, Doran and Co., 1931), pp. 178–179.

[19] Dudley Barker remarks that for *The Glimpse* Bennett "mugged up a theme from Mrs. Besant's theosophical briefs" (*Writer by Trade: A Portrait of Arnold Bennett* [New York: Atheneum, 1966], p. 159). Both the style and the emphasis on mysticism in *The Glimpse* remind one of Mrs. Besant's works. She, of course, was rather learned in the Hindu scriptures as well as Western religious writing, and Bennett was not.

Have Interested Me (1921), he shows some acquaintance with C. M. Doughty, though he considers him difficult. In the *Journal 1929* he speaks of knowing well Saint-Simon and of being enraptured with Rousseau's *Confessions*. All these represent a heterogeneous, indeed motley crew. There was not much in any of them that could supplant the advice of his favorite Stoics.

In his *Journal* note for August 6, 1926, Bennett frankly summed up his frustration. He had been talking with Anita Loos, who "had read philosophy, but had given it up, because she had found it didn't get her anywhere." Bennett appended, as if with annoyance at the philosophers, "This is just my attitude." In "My Religious Experience" he offers a comment that obliquely covers as well his attitude toward philosophy: "One cause of indifference [to religion] was the cautious, agnostic, and self-sufficient bent of my mind."[20] In the same essay he referred to having had a dream of being dead and seeing pennies on his eyelids, but he denied that he had ever believed "the theory set forth" in *The Glimpse*, where he had used the motif.

In that story of 1909 he had created a mélange of mundane incidents and what was intended to represent a mystical vision. He depended heavily on a breathless tone and repeated assertions to convey the mystic experience and to insist that his hero had been transformed spiritually by it. The last words of the book are "But I had seen God." The fact is, however, that the vision is an unconvincing picture of an ideal. Loring has been caught in a net of vexations, small and large, and supposedly he has banished them. But apart from the vision the story is filled with details that make for suspense, and it is with these that Bennett was at home. No assertion of sublimity could

[20] *Things That Have Interested Me: Third Series* (New York: George H. Doran, 1926), pp. 214–215.

let him escape for long from a life which, however romantic, was still earthbound.

If Bennett was not a metaphysician, even in a modest
way, and if his one depiction of mystical experience
sounds like the theatrical sentimentalizing of a singular
dream, he was not, however, devoid of either philosophic
concern or religious feeling. He was always seeking order
and trying to make the mind transcend the material world
with which it was so perpetually occupied. And as for
religion, though he sharply attacked its manifestations in
the Five Towns, he always remained within the shadow of
Wesleyanism, not as a religion of hope and joy, with
optimistic answers, quite the contrary—as one that was
replete with oppressiveness and awesome gloom. He could
castigate hypocrites who professed Methodism; he could
not free himself from the questions it posed. And so he
continued to be puzzled as to the eternal truths and purposes and inclined toward sadness when he contemplated
man's mortal plight.

Yet there were things for the conscious mind to seize
upon that alleviated the autumnal sensation of existence.
Sometimes Bennett's remarks upon them seem to be the
overwelling of a spontaneous pleasure. More often they do
not quite disguise a doggedness of determination to find
life richly worth while. If in *Pilgrim's Progress* Bennett
would have been grouped with those of limited faith, he
would still have earned Bunyan's respect. For without
standing on the exalted peaks and rejoicing in the won-
drous spectacle all about, and with no pretense of having
glimpsed the Celestial City, he did maintain an unflagging
interest in the pathways and the scenery as he journeyed
along.

It was in 1908, in the highly sensible and often exciting
little book *Literary Taste: How to Form It*, that Bennett
wrote, "The makers of literature are those who have seen

and felt the miraculous interestingness of the universe."
Today, when existentialism is a convenient house of a great
many mansions indeed, it is probable that a room could
be found somewhere for Bennett. True, he would have
cringed at being confined even in so airy an apartment
unless it was large enough to accommodate occasional
visits from those obstinate Stoics Epictetus and Marcus
Aurelius. But he did deliberately seek out the interesting, and if it would not fit into a philosophic scheme,
Stoic or other, he would not neglect it. As for the adjective
"miraculous," one can use the word with an abstract
awareness of its appropriateness without feeling oneself
overcome by a miracle. Perhaps it would be most accurate
to suggest that, endowed with more than ordinary sensibility, Bennett diligently cultivated a sense of wonder.
Despite the somewhat exaggerated assertion of his ideal,
however, his actual expectation is probably summed up
by Lord Francis, a minor character in *The Book of Carlotta*,
who remarks to the heroine: "Only the fool and the very
young expect happiness. The wise merely hope to be
interested, at least not to be bored, in their passage through
this world" (103).

Lord Francis concludes with "Nothing is so interesting
as love and grief, and the one involves the other." January 30, 1904, Bennett wrote Miss Lucie Simpson, "I
think there are only two things in this world really worth
having—sexual love & the love of children." [21] Actually a
great many other things intrigued Bennett, too. September
10, 1914, he wrote that he had never before "been so
interested in life." As a consequence of the war, England
was "full of idéas—large general ideas, which overthrow
particular ideas about particular persons." [22] He had
previously asserted in *Clayhanger* that the Dragon hotel in

[21] *Letters of Arnold Bennett*, II, 187.
[22] Letter to Mrs. Elsie Herzog, September 10, 1914 (*Letters*, II, 352).

Bursley was there to remind people of "the interestingness of existence" (19). The Dragon was only one of many microcosms where the human spirit rebelled against a hard, often stultifying fate and sought, crudely, perhaps blindly, for individuality and a bit of pleasure. Music halls were others. Surely they must have grated on Bennett's rather fastidious tastes, and yet he invariably defended their vitality. For the student of life, cheap restaurants were also a diversion, but mainly for a different reason. As haunts for those who could afford better they provided vignettes of lonely, world-weary spirits trying to stifle ennui through mildly sordid distraction.[23] Again one finds parallels, of course, with the works of Balzac, Zola, and especially Huysmans.

In the *Journal* there are several references to the enjoyment of the daily scene in Paris or Fontainebleau or in Burslem. Very often the notes are simple records of immediate sensations. After generalizing about preferring "large spaces, bleak, with simple outlines," Bennett suddenly adds: "On Thursday it rained nearly all day and I walked two hours in the rain. The horse chestnuts in the road are dropping their fruit like heavy ammunition, and people are gathering it for cattle food" (October 5, 1907).[24] A few days later he walked four miles in the rain and noted: "A promenade on a thoroughly bad day in autumn is the next best thing to a promenade on a fine late spring morning. I enjoy it immensely. I enjoy splashing waterproof boots into deep puddles" (October 16, 1907). In Paris it was the busy life of the streets that intrigued

---

[23] As R. A. Scott-James remarks, Bennett was "also aware of the fact that the feeling of intensity and passion may be elicited from a sense of the monotonous, the trivial, and the vapid" (*Personality in Literature: 1913–1931* [New York: Henry Holt, 1932], p. 80).

[24] "The Secret of the Forest," probably of 1904, treats a drive through the forest of Fontainebleau as a romantic adventure (*Things Which Have Interested Me, Third Series* [privately printed, 1908]).

Bennett, in Burslem both the struggles of individuals and the composite impression that resulted from their combined efforts. Even the pall of smoke over Burslem and its sister towns made a romantic spectacle.

Above all, the *Journal* is replete with anecdotes which, often in caricatural intensity, exemplify some human trait or emotion. There is, for example the story of the barmaid who wistfully envied the great dancer Adeline Genée the admiration she received from her audience, but a few minutes later matched the dancer's imperious self-possession when surrounded by her own youthful clientele (January 28, 1899). There is the account by Bennett's landlord and his wife, the Leberts, which showed how quickly and completely people adjust to the shock and degradation of war (November 19, 1907). Bennett was to rely on this reminiscence as a touchstone in *The Old Wives' Tale*. There are stories, too, of misers and other *maniaques*, among whom the most noteworthy was the old, obese, crotchety woman in a Duval restaurant who provided the motif for the narrative of Constance and Sophia Baines (November 18, 1903).

Like others, Bennett was often dismayed by the contemporary industrialism, and yet he found a romantic attraction in the very nature of social and economic organization. The conversion of refuse into electric power in Burslem was a remarkable example of managerial imagination (*Journal*, January, 1906). Railroads were another;[25] and Harrod's store, large hotels, and American skyscrapers involved concepts of business that reached far beyond their own walls. Bennett was to try to convey something of the magnitude of hotel management in *The Imperial Palace* (1930). In *Paris Nights* he lamented his ignorance of the "mysterious people," the miners in the

[25] *Your United States: Impressions of a First Visit* (New York: Harper and Brothers, 1912), p. 99.

Midlands, for here was another world essentially romantic.[26] Underlying every industrial enterprise was the
elemental urge to improve one's standard of living. The
dross, to be sure, was everywhere apparent; greed was to
be assumed, and ugliness was often the immediate consequence. But the reliance of mortal upon mortal and the
ingenuity required for even mediocre success evoked a
sense of wonder. Perhaps the most amazing of all enter-
prises, despite its muddledness, was government. In *Lord
Raingo* (1926), Bennett freely satirized the wartime ministry, and yet the successful prosecution of the war involved
a cooperative sharing of efforts and a determination that
might have been called miraculous. One must be quite
clear on Bennett's view. There was no sentimental maw-
kishness. There was the simple realization that the greater
the social complexity of an action the greater was the
possibility for imaginative creativity.

For Bennett work was virtually synonymous with
creativity, and he repeatedly celebrated it. As we have
noticed, it was, first of all, an escape from ennui. Felix
Babylon buys back the Grand Babylon hotel because he
cannot stand idleness. But he does more than escape from
boredom, for he regains a chance for adventure. George
Cannon in *The Roll Call* (1918) begins to live in yet a new
way when he joins the army. And Lord Raingo needs his
work in the ministry to give him a final short hour of
vitality. What Bennett liked most about America was that
business executives, unlike too many in England, were
"anxious" to get back to their work. Perhaps the two
strongest assertions of his feeling are in *Buried Alive* (1908)
and *The Imperial Palace* (1930). In summing up the

[26] *Paris Nights and Other Impressions of Places and People* (*Essays 1904–1911*)
(New York: George H. Doran, 1913), p. 285. Bennett referred to Zola's
Germinal, on the French mines, as "nearly great," but he considered its
climax "marred by a false sentimentality."

THE SAVOR OF EXISTENCE

thoughts of his artist hero, Priam Farll, he is, of course, also speaking for himself: "Like every ageing artist of genuine accomplishment, he knew—none better—that there is no satisfaction save the satisfaction of fatigue after honest endeavour."[27] Orcham in *The Imperial Palace* is to have several adventures that for a while distract him from the management of the luxury hotel, but both at the beginning and at the end of his history he realizes that it is the problems he faces at the office that give him his very reason for continuing to exist: "He needed them. They exhilarated him. They were his life. Without them he would have sunk into tedium" (45). Naturally, for Bennett himself there was a far greater adventure in writing *The Old Wives' Tale* or *Clayhanger* than in spinning out *A Great Man* or *Teresa of Watling Street*.

Next best to writing, and a fine stimulation toward it, was indulgence in the society of artists. While he was working regularly at *Clayhanger* Bennett recorded in his *Florentine Journal*, April 16, 1910, the excitement of a discussion at the home of his Hungarian friend Odon Por: "What a contrast, in their freedom, wit, and taste in art, and their enthusiasm, from the dreadful dull social atmosphere of this excellent but damned pension."[28] After spending four hours one evening with artists at a Parisian café, he recorded with excusable hyperbole: "I saw in my imagination the vista of the thousands of similar nights which my friends had spent, and the vista of the thousands of similar nights which they would spend. And the sight was majestic, tremendous."[29]

When Mr. Prohack is forced by fragile health to become a gentleman of leisure he is advised to work at being idle. The advice, like the other observations in the novel, seems

---

[27] *Buried Alive* (London: Methuen and Co., 1960), p. 157.
[28] *Florentine Journal* (London: Chatto and Windus, 1967).
[29] "Evening with Exiles," in *Paris Nights*, p. 37.

to reflect Bennett's own view. Even idleness had its discipline. For Mr. Prohack there is virtue in deliberate
waste; for his creator there was likewise virtue in culti-
vating a life of leisure. Of course, he had to do so almost
as if by stealth, because even on his various yachting
excursions he was writing hard and gathering substance
for later books. Yet he did value what he so seldom for long
allowed himself, and it is pleasant to find him asserting
with boyish naïveté that when the "Velsa" came into port
at Dordrecht "I wanted the best tea, and here I got it."[30]
Not the money, but the trouble involved was pure extrava-
gance. Still it was indispensable for the exquisite savoring
of life. Significantly, it was when he himself was about
fifty years old that, in *Buried Alive*, Bennett gave his hero
that age and called it "the most romantic and tender of
all ages—for a male" (11).

In his *Experiment in Autobiography* H. G. Wells sums up
Bennett's approach to his world:

> Bennett was taking the thing that is, for what it was, with
> a naïve and eager zest. He saw it brighter than it was;
> he did not see into it and he did not see beyond it. He
> was like a child at a fair. His only trouble was how to get
> everything in in the time at his disposal, music, pictures,
> books, shows, eating, drinking, display, the remarkable
> clothes one could wear, the remarkable stunts one could
> do, the unexpected persons, the incessant fresh oddities
> of people; the whole adorable, incessant, multitudinous
> lark of it.[31]

The portrait is, of course, incomplete, for Wells was
judging not from the serious novels, but from personal

[30] *From the Log of the Velsa* (New York: The Century Co., 1914), p. 90.
[31] H. G. Wells, *Experiment in Autobiography* (New York: Macmillan, 1934),
p. 535. Wells goes on to say, "The bright clear mosaic of impressions was
continually being added to and all the pieces stayed in their places. He did
not feel the need for a philosophy or for a faith or for anything to hold them
together" (536).

impressions. Yet it is not without justification. There is a great deal in the *Journal* and elsewhere on the phantasmagoria of life.

Apropos of *The Book of Carlotta* Wells wrote Bennett in 1905, "You are always taking surface values that I reject, hotels are not luxuries, *trains de luxe* are full of coal grit, *chefs* and pianists are not marvelous persons, dramatic triumphs are silly uproars." To this charge Bennett replied: "You will never see it, but in rejecting surface values you are wrong. As a fact they are just as important as other values."[32] Sometimes it does seem as if Bennett were saying that the surface of things was the reality and that one could build an orderly concept of existence by finding a pattern in the surface itself. Really, however, his view was by no means so simple. The externals were certainly the material with which the mind must work; but the pattern was still a private creation for the individual mind. A miser might appear to be merely obsessed with the possession of money, but even miserliness had its own principles, as Bennett was to reveal in *Riceyman Steps*. As for himself, he was not lacking in concern for a design.

Wells was interested in remolding the world; Bennett was much more preoccupied with self-discipline. As a follower, albeit inconsistent, of Marcus Aurelius and Epictetus, he tried to make the conscious mind prevail. This meant building some kind of ideal concept of oneself and establishing its dominance over recalcitrant circumstance. Of course, the question that remains is how good a design Bennett achieved. Certainly the recommendations of his two philosophers were more negative than positive, and the mental order which one establishes may be only

[32] *Arnold Bennett and H. G. Wells: A Record of a Personal and Literary Friendship*, ed. Harris Wilson (Urbana: University of Illinois Press, 1960), pp. 121 and 125. The exchange was September 25 and September 30, 1905.

illusory. Bennett himself wanted to have a rigorous, consciously disciplined view of existence and, at the same time, to enjoy its fullness. The two efforts, often so contrary, may be the basis of Wells's sweeping judgment. In addition, as we have seen, there was always that lurking sense of malaise which no act of conscious will could allay. The consequence is that, although Bennett did not arrive at a unifying philosophy, he was not without a loose bundle of principles by which he tried to live and think.

More important, he was not without self-knowledge. In one of the earliest entries in the *Journal*, December 9, 1896, he speaks of the "proud, self-conscious self-esteem" of his family, and he continues, "We are of the North, outwardly brusque, stoical, undemonstrative, scornful of the impulsive; inwardly all sentiment and crushed tenderness." Here was an honest admission of the superiority of the heart over the stubborn head. In a *Journal* note more than eleven years later, May 23, 1908, Bennett is dismayed at his shortcomings in mental discipline:

> Yet I have gradually got my brain far better under control than most people. Always haunted by dissatisfaction at the discrepancy between reason and conduct! No reason why conduct should not conform to the ideas of reason except inefficient control of the brain. This that I am always preaching, and with a success of popular interest too, I cannot perfectly practise. It is the clumsiness of my living that disgusts me. The rough carpentry instead of fine cabinetry.

The *Journal* and the personal memoirs by Marguerite and Dorothy Cheston Bennett support Newman Flower's remark that Bennett "lived by schedule, worked by schedule, and ate by schedule." [33] Sometimes when the schedule

[33] Newman Flower, *Just as It Happened* (London: Cassell, 1950), p. 158.

was quite arbitrary one suspects that Bennett was desperately imposing a semblance of order rather than its
reality.

The pocket philosophies contrast reason and sentiment,
to the advantage of reason. Typical is a passage in *The
Human Machine* (1909): "The brain is always more kind
than the heart; . . . the brain always does the difficult,
unselfish thing, and the heart always does the facile,
showy thing" (119). Increasingly with time Bennett
equates reason with the masculine mind and sentiment
with the feminine heart. Thus, in *Our Women: Chapters on
the Sex-Discord* (1920), he unchivalrously asserts, "And the
truth is that intellectually and creatively man is the
superior of women."[34] A few pages later he pushes the
issue: "Superior intellectual power means, and always did
mean, domination" (116). And in a rather trite summary
he repeats his argument: "Jack leans towards reason. Jill
leans towards sentiment" (117). In this and other books
he does temporize by crediting women with the greater
"will power, and tenacity or perseverance" (123).[35]

In *How to Make the Best of Life* (1923), Bennett remarks
most pointedly that "a man who finds his existence full
and interesting, an ambitious man, will not fall in love."[36]
In *The Imperial Palace*, though eventually Orcham is to be
satisfactorily married, at the outset he feels that marriage
to an attractive woman would be disorganizing, and before
he finally reaches his marital haven he experiences to the
point of surfeit what he has feared, for Gracie shatters his

[34] *Our Women: Chapters on the Sex-Discord* (New York: George H. Doran,
1920), p. 112.
[35] Mrs. Dorothy Cheston Bennett finds a "false note" in Bennett's portrayal of women, and she considers it "prompted, fundamentally, by a
criticism or a dislike of the female sex that no amount of flattering descriptions conceal" (*Arnold Bennett: A Portrait Done at Home* [New York: Kendall
and Sharp, 1935], p. 118).
[36] *How to Make the Best of Life* (New York: George H. Doran, 1923), p. 101.

orderly world. One comment in *Our Women* expresses the age-worn view refurbished by Zola in *L'Oeuvre* that women consider a man's art their major rival. The complaint is made concrete in "The Cornet Player," [37] where the wife, upon becoming a mother, casts her musician-husband's horn into the bushes. In all the allusions to the conflict of head and heart and even in the playful contests of will between husband and wife that make up the plots of several stories the role of reason is really not to achieve a philosophic transcendance of circumstance, but rather to coerce it into a mold. In her portrait of her husband, Dorothy Cheston Bennett writes:

> In his personal or domestic relations, especially in 1923 and 1924, he makes me think of a gardener who had long ago determined to keep nature in order and see that plants should grow where, and if, and how, they were planted. If they did not grow so, he felt that reasonable discourse ought to show them the way to. (106)

It is only a step from preoccupation with order to the establishing of a personal role. Punctuality, for example, became for Bennett an obsession. He repeatedly notes the time of departure and arrival, and if he or one of his characters goes to the theater, he must be neither late nor more than five minutes early. A walk is not about an hour long; it is fifty-nine minutes long (*Journal*, October 16, 1907). Just as he liked the near magic that permitted a large organization to function, so he wanted the routine of his own daily existence to be crisply efficient. He was concerned about the boiling of an egg and the brewing of tea, the position of a table or chair, and the acceptable decibels of a duck's quack. It was not really that life was more

[37] Published in *The Night Visitor and Other Stories* (New York: Doubleday, Doran and Co., 1931).

comfortable when all had been subjected to system. It was rather that somehow the conscious mind had won a victory. There are many stubborn characters in Bennett's fiction; some are caricatures, and all are treated with amusement. It seems as if in laughing at them Bennett was having fun with his own excesses.

Role-playing reached its climax, of course, in Bennett's own personal manners and urbanity. He clearly felt that the cultivation of his personal identity was a creative art. [38] Actually the picture he gives of himself in his autobiographic writing is not flattering, for he tried to be quite honest. Where there is exaggeration it is in the spirit of *The Card*, and any boasting is singularly unegoistic. It is mainly a glorification of *savoir-faire*. In *The Truth about an Author* Bennett was willing to play down his seriousness as a writer to play up his knowingness in the workshop of letters. He unabashedly emphasized the speed with which he could scan and review books. In that work and elsewhere he was facile in offhand remarks about music and art. In *Things That Have Interested Me (Second Series)* (1923), he announced, "For a rank amateur I have had vast experience of listening to music." [39] He was likely to make a dogmatic statement on no foundation whatever, as, when speaking of Lilian's large mouth, he says it is "the certain sign of goodwill and understanding in a woman." [40] Indeed, many of his remarks about women are meant to imply that he was an expert in female psychology.

In the novels, particularly the fantasias, much is made of the masterfulness with which clever young women and

---

[38] In an introduction to *The Old Wives' Tale* Somerset Maugham wrote, "I feel that to [Bennett] life itself was a rôle he played conscientiously, and with ability, but into the skin of which he never quite got" (Reprinted in "Arnold Bennett," *Life and Letters*, VI [1931], 422).

[39] *Things That Have Interested Me (Second Series)* (London: Chatto and Windus, 1923), p. 188.

[40] *Lilian* (New York: George H. Doran, 1922), p. 39.

men of consequence get their wishes. Typical is the remark in *The Lion's Share* (1916) that Mr. Gilman is a "truly great expert" in "giving a meal in a restaurant." [41] The nadir of urbanity is exposed here and there in the fiction and is recorded with naïve condemnation in the *Journal*. Having, for example, attended a committee meeting concerned with the care of wounded soldiers, Bennett afterward jotted down, "It lasted from 5 to 7.35, and Lord Swaything kept relighting *one* cigar the whole time" (May 13, 1915).

Your United States (1912), which records Bennett's adventures on a visit across the Atlantic, is perhaps the only example of naïve condescension. That he found much to deplore during his sojourn is not astonishing, though some of his annoyances were trivial; what does disturb is his tone of approbation, as if his American readers might feel more secure each time he stamped his approval on what he saw. And though residents of the city might be pleased, his casual visit in Indianapolis hardly gave him the right to pronounce it "the present chief center of letters in the United States" (65).

By 1929 many of the comments in the *Journal*—including *Journal 1929*—have to do with personal service in hotels, wines, cigars, fashionable restaurants, yachts, and such other paraphernalia as should accommodate the man of cultivated tastes who also attends the theater and concerts and frequents art galleries. Along with the remarks, sometimes self-deprecating, that characterize a man of the world, there are other comments no less revealing. October 31, 1926, for example, Mrs. Bennett and Bennett met the nurse with Virginia in Hyde Park. First Bennett notes that both parties were punctual. He continues, "Dorothy wanted to know whether I felt it was 'undignified' for me to walk by the perambulator in the crowded Sunday

41 *The Lion's Share* (London: Cassell, n.d.), p. 302.

morning Park! I did, however, refuse to push the vehicle myself." Could anything be more charmingly boyish? The conscious mind could master things; it could even map out a pattern for existence and pose an ideal image of oneself; it could not be trusted to retain control when the springs of one's self-conscious being were at work.

Rebecca West, with oversimplification, to be sure, insisted that the image which Bennett tried to create was really inspired by shyness: "I have told how he built up an impersonation of a comic personality—stiff-limbed, dogmatic, imperturbable—as a defense behind which to hide."[42] J. B. Atkins calls Bennett "more naïve than worldly-wise. . . . To him the world of comfort with the pleasures that money could buy was a wonderful discovery. It was like a toy to a child . . . ."[43] And Dorothy Cheston Bennett writes, "I think that the machinery and contrivances of life were to him the toy-boats, the railway lines and signalling apparatus, which in his boyhood he had never possessed."[44]

There was one incident in Bennett's life which seems to have bothered him not a little—a railway accident July 7, 1911, at Nantes. It merely reveals in heightened form something that one senses frequently in the *Journal*. Bennett wrote about it in the *Journal* the next day and in a letter to Mrs. Wells and at least twice in print, and then he significantly transformed it several years later in the light novel *Accident* (1929). In the *Journal* he spoke quite frankly and egoistically of his deliberate efforts to stay uninvolved: "I had no desire of any sort to help. I argued incompassionately that it was the incompetent railway company's affairs. . . . I didn't want to see any more

[42] Rebecca West, *Arnold Bennett Himself* (The John Day Pamphlets, 1931), p. 20.
[43] Atkins, *Incidents and Reflections*, p. 175.
[44] D. C. Bennett, *Arnold Bennett*, p. 24.

wounded nor to be any more *impressioné* than I could help."
To Mrs. Wells he again noted as in the *Journal* his ingenuity in immediately hiring an automobile and selling
three places in it so that, despite the accident, he arrived
in Paris "only a quarter of an hour late for dinner!"[45] In
Things That Have Interested Me (1921), he indicated that
he was shaken and flustered and he implied that it was
because he would have been useless in rescue work that
he rushed to Paris.[46] In the fictitious version Alan Frith-
Walter is not heroic after the accident; instead, the sophisticated young Pearl takes over with perfect aplomb. But
Frith-Walter is only for a moment an egoist. In the
Journal the egoism is slightly mitigated by a hint that all
was not really well with the man who scurried away to
Paris. One suspects that when the accident had receded
into the corridors of the past Bennett was much more
aware that being almost punctual for dinner was a weak
substitute for facing the true event. Though he was a
disciple of the Goncourts, a student of Zola and Moore,
and a portrayer in his own fiction of the decline and death
of men and women, his conscious mind could not steel
him to face the unpleasant reality. It certainly did not
guide him as he felt it should to an infallible choice.

In fact, Bennett could not with any fairness to himself
pretend that the subconscious and inexplicable motiva-
tions of human action were not the primary substance of
existence, however refractory they were in any rationally
imposed scheme of things. Sophia Baines may consciously
refuse to accompany Gerald Scales to Paris as an unmarried woman, but this and all other decisions which
keep her in the path of conventional morality stem from
her emotional sensitivity. To make one choice may lead to

---

[45] *Arnold Bennett and H. G. Wells*, July 8, pp. 177–178.
[46] *Things That Have Interested Me* (New York: George H. Doran, 1921),
pp. 96–98.

a rather bleak, arid existence, but the alternative is an
affront to her sensibilities. Again and again in the *Journal*
and other works one is acutely conscious of Bennett's
own temperament. In *How to Make the Best of Life*, a book
rather packed with truisms, he admitted that man is only
"sometimes a reasoning animal," and that he is "a tem-
peramental animal all the time" (9). He added that "no
man can change his temperament" (10). Of course, he
soon returned to his set position that it was the function
of reasoning to keep one's temperament "in order" (12).

For daily fare Bennett was content with the savor of
small incidents and scenes. In *The Love Match* Hugh Russ
remarks that "life's very daily," and that it "wants a lot
of small change."[47] Bennett felt this was so, and he tried
to justify his belief by the argument that "the biggest
things in life depend on the smallest things."[48] He sought
to find universal issues in the frustrations of little people—
a Constance Baines or a Clerkenwell miser. When he put
together *Mediterranean Scenes* (1928), he was as much preoccupied as ever with his sensation of the things immediately before him—the dust, the flies, the bazaars, the
costumes. Though he generalized about other matters, he
was quite contented merely to record these with at most a
quip to fit them into a not-very-large frame. The senses
responded to them and the conscious mind described them.
They existed and so they were to be reckoned with. No
further justification was needed.

At the same time, Bennett had his beliefs. Those that
mattered concerned one's relations with his fellow men,
and the most wonderful relationship involved the attraction between men and women. In that attraction there
was romance because there was mystery; the imagination

[47] *The Love Match: A Play in Five Scenes* (New York: George H. Doran,
1922), p. 110.
[48] *How to Make the Best of Life*, p. 97.

was teased into a pitch of activity that lifted one out of the dailiness of life. Again Bennett stops well short of the ecstatic. His language is never that of an idealizer of women. His feeling is epitomized in his description of a statue in the National Museum at Athens. In looking at various statues he had been more concerned with their human interest than with their artistic excellence. Then he came upon one of a young woman—a reproduction painted in lifelike tones—and he forgot all about art to apostrophize her as a very earthly woman who "must have been a handful for some man . . . . You have the thrill which nothing of the golden age in these rooms has yet given you." [49]

Bennett also, though far more rarely, could describe a disillusionment that went beyond the ordinary dissatisfaction of a critical observer. In giving Orcham's sensations at the Caligula bar and dance hall, in *The Imperial Palace*, he voiced his own revulsion:

> What a crew (thought Evelyn)! Foolish faces, lascivious, abandoned, inane. How grotesquely indecent the faces of the old men in the sweltering crowd! How hard, insincere, grasping, or sentimental and sensually loving, the faces of the girls. All pretending joy, in the hope of satisfactions to come! All utterly despicable! He was ashamed to be there . . . . (493)

Several years earlier, in *Our Women* (1920), Bennett had written that he would like for his epitaph "He tried to destroy illusions" (67). The words seem to protest too much, and there is a great deal in Bennett's writing that they do not fit. Perhaps, however, it would be correct to conclude that he himself was at times acutely disillusioned.

[49] *Mediterranean Scenes: Rome-Greece-Constantinople* (London: Cassell, 1928), p. 57.

The Imperial Palace, Bennett's last major work, stretches to 769 pages. Though not so fine as a number of earlier works, it was a colossal and exhausting undertaking. With determination and apparently with enthusiasm its author saw his task through. He had the satisfaction of immersing himself in minute details because they attracted his imagination and also of making reason prevail by imposing order upon a great mass of substance. Thus to a degree he gave expression to both his temperament and his Stoic sense of mental discipline. But along the way he emitted an unusual cry of anguish. The context before and after tends to soften its effect, yet it is intense enough. Orcham at the opera with the world-weary Gracie is himself suffering from ennui. Bennett does not stop with a simple statement of Orcham's feelings. Instead, attributing to him thoughts that sound strikingly autobiographical, he suggests that he might have gone on to reflect, "Why are we anywhere? Why is anything? Is there after all a key to the preposterous enigma of the universe?" (478). Two hundred and ninety-one pages later Orcham accepts his existence, but Bennett has been able to provide him only oblique hints of an answer.

CHAPTER TWO

The Prospect of a Wilderness

WHY SHOULD IT matter what Arnold Bennett happened to say about the politics, industry, home life, culture, or religion of his times? For generations writers had been recording the shortcomings of society. What could Bennett present that had not been put wittily by Swift or Fielding, or more recently by Thackeray, or with moral indignation by Dickens, or with sober reflection by George Eliot, Mrs. Gaskell, and innumerable journalists? If one is looking only for generic matters, the answer is "Little enough." If one asks whether Bennett studied his predecessors before launching upon his own panoramic depiction, the answer, again, is "Not very much." He knew them, of course; two or three times, for example, he mentions *A Tale of a Tub*, and, despite his professed dislike for Dickens, he is now and then almost Dickensian. But the only author whom he seems to have valued highly for his representation of the social scene was Balzac, and there is a vast difference between Bennett's subjects and those of his French master.

Consequently we find him traversing afresh old pathways without benefiting much from the travelogues of his
predecessors. He attacks hypocrisy, cultural sterility, and
wrongheadedness as if they had never been assaulted
before. Just the same, there is a difference. The ancient
ills were still abroad in the 1890's and early 1900's, but
their avatars wore new clothing. More important, man's
perspectives had changed. In Bennett we find a point of
view that is transitional, inclining decidedly toward the
very modern. When they treat of the same topics, such as
the position of women, he is in accord with Meredith and
Thomas Hardy; but even then his women's problems are
somewhat altered from those of an Aminta Ormont or a
Sue Bridehead.

As for his originality among his contemporaries—here
we have to deal mainly with Galsworthy and Wells and
with the journals and newspapers of the time. It is impossible to say when Bennett is pioneering and when he is
developing a hint which he has come across somewhere.
What we can do is ascertain the convictions which he came
to hold and often to emphasize. In so doing we get an
insight into the life of the times as it appeared to one
sensitive contemporary mind.

Bennett seems to have had only a moderate interest in
politics and government per se, and usually he fused
political issues with other matters. Even Lord Raingo is,
first of all, a bewildered human being, and we are more
interested in his private frustrations than in the bumbling
of the ministry for which he works. Much of Bennett's
political commentary is in light satire, at times almost
playful, yet with troublesome overtones. A good example
is in *London Life* (1924) by Bennett and Edward Knoblock.
Simon Blackshaw has risen to the ministry and at the
same time has profited financially. He is not guilty of
outright dishonesty, and yet he regrets having deserted his

democratic ideals by becoming a "champion of low taxes for the rich" and getting "a bit of unearned increment" through methods that he "didn't care to own." He bewails the degradation of politics: "The humiliations, the disappointments, the subterfuges, the ingratitude, the disgusting compromises, the chicane, the damned rascalities—." Still, Simon is nothing if not in politics, and so at the end of the play he is preparing an election address: "We must try again to be honest. Ideals are worth living for. Nothing else is. We must stick to our ideals."[1] The play is farcical, and the audience is not given time to reflect on the fundamental evils; but there is a whimsical absurdity in Simon's preparing to immerse himself once more in a murky whirlpool, protected only by his naïve illusions.

In *Clayhanger* the attack is centered on the campaigners. Edwin is disgusted with their cynical contempt for the voters they seek to deceive. In *Lord Raingo* the demagoguery extends into Parliament, where the backbenchers are "sheep, scurrying forward at the onrush and yelp of the trained dog!"[2] The main satire in the latter novel concerns the ministries caught up in a war on the Continent while carrying on their popgun battles among themselves. The most farcical ridicule concerns an expert on France who is trying to cement ties with the French by setting up committees throughout France to reassure its citizens that the British, too, are interested in landscape gardening. More realistic is the justification for Sir Rupert Afflock's becoming secretary for war. Sir Rupert is an expert on many things nonmilitary: "Hence, in accordance with the British tradition against employing experts in the high offices of state, he had been made Secretary of State for War" (194). Though much of the

[1] Bennett and Edward Knoblock, *London Life: A Play in Three Acts and Nine Scenes* (New York: George H. Doran, 1924), pp. 164, 165, 171.
[2] *Lord Raingo* (New York: George H. Doran, 1926), p. 86.

commentary is good-natured—and Winston Churchill
particularly liked what he considered a caricature of himself—there is a mixture, in perhaps equal parts, of wonder
at the very possibility of men's working together in a
magnificent social adventure and of wry amusement at
their absurdities.

For Sam Raingo political position and social prestige
are linked; he must become a lord, no matter how petty
and insincere the conniving required. In 1918 in a comedy
The Title, Bennett had laughed at the notion of honors
lists, yet had not been severe on Culver for accepting a
title. Now, in the novel, Raingo, who ought to be absorbed
with his work, becomes instead busied with such trivial
details as "notepaper, envelopes, crests, coat-of-arms"
(160). At the ceremony he is a doll helplessly set in motion
by others. Bennett sums up: "Sam felt at once an ass, a
cynic and a conqueror" (162).

The most unqualified of Bennett's condemnations refer
to the legal system. In *Whom God Hath Joined* (1906), the
antiquated divorce laws are not only unjust; they seem
maliciously inspired to humiliate victims. The attack is
perhaps more savage than Hardy's in *Jude the Obscure*
because the very atmosphere of the courtroom and the
machinery of the process for securing a divorce are
shocking to the sensibilities. Indeed Bennett dramatizes
the proceedings as a tragic nightmare.[3] Seventeen years
later, in "Guilty till Proved Innocent," he again unleashed
his indignation: "A great deal of our legal system is
totally barbaric. It is not merely unjust. It is infamous."[4]

As for his own politics, Bennett was a socialist, but with
no great faith in socialist doctrine. In his *Journal* for November 20, 1907, he notes for a possible article the topic

[3] The general topic was suggested to Bennett by a publisher. Cf. Dudley
Barker, *Writer by Trade*, p. 118.

[4] *Things That Have Interested Me* (*Second Series*), p. 121.

"The Individualism of Socialism," in which he might consider "the fact that all political questions, such as those which agitate socialists, are simply questions of machinery—and do not directly touch the question of living (intensely)." In *Buried Alive*, published a few months later, he has fun with the socialistic fad. Farll overhears a man say: "Socialism is the thing just now. Read Wells on Socialism. It'll be all over the theatrical world in a few years time" (52). In *Clayhanger*, Edwin votes Labour "defiantly," and mutters to himself, "I'll be more out-and-out Radical than ever!" (446, 451); but nothing significant results from his pique.

On one political issue Bennett took a determined stand —rearmament. In "The Fourth Armistice Day," he called rearming a plainly marked "way to catastrophe" along which "we travel fatalistically straight forward."[5] Though certainly by no means novel, his admonition was no mere echo of the voices of others, and its aptness was to be demonstrated.

All in all, Bennett's political views were not central to his commentaries on the age. Though he knew Mill and Spencer, he chose to present, not a theory, but a few observations on the shortcomings of the traditional governmental system and the vanities and frustrations of individual political leaders. His sketches depict aridity of imagination and muddleheadedness. Except for the few sharp thrusts they have what might be called a Prohackian generosity. That is—and especially in *Lord Raingo*—the vanities are laughed at, but the culprits are forgiven because they are, after all, no more fallible than the rest of mankind.

Industrial matters were rather more within Bennett's range of experience and interest than were the political, since he came from a community of mines, potteries, and

[5] *Ibid.*, p. 182.

factories. Extraordinarily methodical in his own business
affairs, he was unhappy about the industrial inefficiency
he found in the Midlands. In *Leonora* (1903) Arthur blames
Five-Towns industrialists for holding to "old-fashioned
methods,"[6] a lament to be reiterated in *Clayhanger* seven
years later, and again in *Milestones* in 1912. In *Whom God
Hath Joined* the backwardness of Five-Towns offices is
measured by the fact that typewriters and speaking tubes
are innovations in a business street "overawed by tory-
ism."[7] In "The British Home," Bennett summed up his
complaint, "The average office and the average works are
emphatically not run on business lines, except in theory."[8]

A year earlier, in *Your United States*, he had expressed
his surprise and delight that American businessmen were
enthusiastic about their work. In *The Plain Man and His
Wife* (1913), in contrast, he protested that most British
businessmen found their work irksome and pursued it only
for financial gain. Perhaps the best statement of the issues
is some seventeen years later, in *The Imperial Palace*.
Orcham is ambivalent about a merger. Though under
present conditions the workers are and must remain ill
paid, the change will immediately worsen matters by
depriving a number of them of any employment. But Sir
Henry defends a transition that will bring specialized
repetitive work and, with it, lower prices. He admits that
there will be displacement of workers, but insists that
there must be improved mechanism. Bennett was certainly
not indifferent to the deadening effects of mere repetition.
Especially in *Clayhanger* he had deplored the stultifying
labor of the factory girls. But the trouble that had existed
in the days when Darius Clayhanger refused to build a
modern plant and which was still too prevalent in 1931

[6] *Leonora: A Novel* (New York: George H. Doran, 1910), p. 93.
[7] *Whom God Hath Joined* (New York: n.d.), pp. 70–71.
[8] *Paris Nights*, p. 333.

was that the sheer inefficiency was also stultifying. It was possible through modernization to give respect to a worker by making him feel productive. There could be no defense for onerous chores, however diversified. Where there had never been an opportunity for creativeness by the laborers, it was at least a gain to eliminate meaningless drudgery and achieve efficiency. In short, Bennett was not one to insist on a utopia where, somehow every workman was to revel in creative joy. He was dealing with plain men in an actual world. Workmen would seldom be innovative in any event; and it devolved upon industrial management to eliminate waste, improve physical working conditions, and achieve a better product. Only thus could the standard of living for everyone be raised.

Not entirely separate from his concern for industrial inefficiency was Bennett's dissatisfaction with the class relationships in England. Essentially he limited his discussion to the middle class—which might include the rich—and the poor, primarily servants and unskilled or semiskilled industrial workers. The latter were not without fault, but the senseless perpetration of cruelty and injustice could be charged against their middle-class employers, more accurately, perhaps, their economic and social masters.

What Bennett had already been saying, often obliquely, he put most emphatically in 1909 in an essay, "The Novel-Reading Public," which stressed not only the cultural, but the moral blindness of the middle class. Treating its "sincere religious worship of money and financial success" as a truism, he attacked its self-conscious "grim passion for the status quo," a passion manifested in a "general defensive sullen hatred of all ideas whatever."[9] In the fiction he was able to descend to specific examples. When he did, the implied commentary

[9] Hynes, *The Author's Craft*, pp. 76–77.

is accentuated by the fact that the worst sinners are very
nice, well-intentioned persons. Leonora, the heroine of
the novel named for her (1903), is an example. She earns
our sympathy because she is herself the product of the
social traditions that are now crushing her spirit. Unfortunately, in her longing for personal freedom, she is
oblivious of her role in the crushing of others:

> All around was grime, squalor, servitude, ugliness; the
> inglorious travail of two hundred thousand people, above
> ground and below it, filled the day and the night. But
> here, as it were suddenly, out of that earthy and labor-
> ious bed, rose the blossom of luxury, grace, and leisure,
> the final elegance of the industrial district of the Five
> Towns. . . . She felt that the loud-voiced girls [in the
> archway] were at one extremity of the scale and she at
> the other; and this arrangement seemed natural,
> necessary, inevitable. (5–6)

In a *Journal* entry, January 2, 1908, Bennett called
London "a city of very rich and very poor." In Bond Street
he was struck with the "physical arrogance" of the rich,
"well-groomed, physically fit male animal." Two days
later he followed up with the note "It is almost disconcerting to think that all this vast idle class has to 'go' one
day. The idlers in this hotel make an imposing array.
Offensive, many of them." Two years later, January 2,
1910, Bennett recorded his pleasure in strolling along the
front at Brighton. Then he continued: "But I am obsessed
by the thought that all this comfort, luxury, ostentation,
snobbishness, and correctness, is founded on a vast injustice to the artisan class." A few days later, January 11,
he returned to the issue:

> Certainly this morning as I looked at all the splendid
> solidity of Brighton, symbol of a system that is built on

the grinding of the faces of the poor, I had to admit that
it would take a lot of demolishing, that I couldn't expect
to overset it with a single manifesto and a single election,
or with 50.

Sometime during the next few weeks Bennett gave Clayhanger a similar distress as he contrasted the affluent and
the wretched at Brighton. These are his most nearly
explicit expressions of socialism. They are, of course,
negative, only pointing to the ills without suggesting how
they were to be corrected.

In Bennett's last major work, *The Imperial Palace*,
Orcham is disturbed by the fact that the women guests
revel in silken luxury only because the women servants rise
early, put their own homes in order, walk a mile or two to
the hotel, and then begin "swilling and dusting like the
devil" (39). Gracie, herself an idle rich girl, contrasts the
workers with the "greedy rotters" who frequent the
fashionable restaurant (116). The sharpest commentary
on the absurdity of idle luxury is Orcham's genuine pity
for the hotel patrons: "They pressed magic buttons, and
their caprices were instantly gratified. But to Evelyn they
were as touching as the piteous figures crouching and
shivering in the lamp-lit night on the benches of the
Thames Embankment" (129).

The general coal strike began February 26, 1912.
March 4, Bennett recorded in his *Journal* the reaction of
Mrs. Julia Frankau: "Of course I'm feudal. I'd batten
them down. I'd make them work. They *should* work. I'd
force them down." He took up the matter again March 23
and noted that he "must have a strike in [his] continental
novel." He had occasion to refurbish Mrs. Frankau's
words in *These Twain*, four years later. There the friends
of a colliery owner assume that a strike is the work of
"mischievous demagogues," and a young girl exclaims,

"The leaders ought to be shot, and the men who won't go down the pits ought to be *forced* to go down and *made* to work" (305). A page later Bennett points the irony: "It was an ideal world, full of ideal beings."

Again, as in *Leonora*, he brings the matter down to the specific case. Clayhanger is progressive in modernizing his lithographic establishment, but he is uneasy because even it will be "one of the prisons, one of the money-works" for exploiting the poor (314). And why? So that Hilda can enjoy luxuries. Edwin Clayhanger would never perpetuate the cruelty of his father, Darius, for whom the workers were soulless drudges. Still he asks a boy to add a half hour to an already overlong day, with no thought of the sacrifice he is demanding from the lad and his mother. As for a typical girl in Edwin's shop, "she was the slave of the machine" (230). Yet Edwin is the most enlightened of all Bennett's industrialists.

Bennett supported women's suffrage primarily because of his concern for women who had to work. His *Journal* note on Christmas Eve, 1908, is scornful of women who were ashamed of the suffragettes and maintained that women should remain in the home: "(It is incredible how people still talk.) I then burst out impatiently: 'Yes, and what about the millions of them that have to leave home every day to earn a living? What about the mill girls, and the typists?' This quite unsettled them" (311).

At about the same time Bennett was working on *The Glimpse*. Besides attacking the dreariness of middle-class life and the "enormity of the physical apparatus" with which it "encumbered mere existence," he joined the tradition of those who throughout the Victorian decades had decried piecework enslavement: "And I saw another ring of homes where a gross of boxes were made for a farthing, and two shirts for ten farthings, and where a woman might work for a hundred hours and not earn enough to buy a porterhouse steak."[10] In *Paris Nights* (1913) he again lamented the drudgery of women clerks and of other women working in garrets so that, with no reservation of conscience, yet other women could be expensively attired. Having made the point in one essay, he returned to it in another in the same volume:

> In nearly all public places of pleasure, the pleasure is poisoned for me by the obsession that I owe it, at last, to the underpaid labour of people who aren't there and can't be there; by the growing, deepening obsession that the whole structure of what a respectable person means, when he says with patriotic warmth "England," is reared on a stupendous and shocking injustice. (278–279)[11]

Three years after the armistice Bennett saw some improvement in the British schools, but he still found their curricula archaic. He urged as an important topic of study the "Enslavement of the Working Classes and the Struggle for Freedom."[12] He was not a starry-eyed reformer. In *Clayhanger* he had shown that laboring men could waste their income on drink, and in *Hilda Lessways* the quarreling strikers "had swung back a hundred centuries towards original crude life" (510). But putting together his pleas for better wages and his deploring of the artificiality and fatuous luxuries of the middle class, one can conclude that what he wanted was for the laboring men and women to earn a living by performing—with specialization when possible—those tasks which would contribute to a comfortable existence with something to spare for the amenities. It is, of course, uncertain how easily he himself could have foregone habits that were far from Spartan, but perhaps

[10] *The Glimpse: An Adventure of the Soul* (New York: 1909), pp. 21–22.

[11] In *The Lion's Share* (1916) the suffragette Jane Foley points out the discriminations against women as to salary and working conditions in the mills.

[12] "Teaching History," in *Things That Have Interested Me*, p. 149.

he could defend himself on the ground that he toiled hard at his writing and that even the maintenance of a yacht contributed to his efficiency.

Regarding himself as a craftsman, Bennett naturally wanted as many workmen as possible to take pride in their skills; and, like Galsworthy and a good many others, he felt that artisanship was waning. In "The Limits of Dominion" he summarizes Mr. Furber's lecture to his son: "It was the dour, obstinate expression of dying ideals, of the artisan's deep and narrow pride and prejudice, of a conviction that labour had a prestige surpassing that of capital."[13] Such a spirit was to be protected even in the process of mechanization and specialization in the mills. Bennett did not, however, suggest how.

Nor was he always consistent in his feelings toward the working class. In a "burst of fellowship" he had once shaken hands with a carpenter, who always thereafter, on their meeting, repeated the ceremony. One day as he was leaving, Bennett impulsively evaded the handshake. His *Journal* for September 14, 1909, records his perplexity: "A decent, independent chap, vigorous and energetic. Young. What is at the back of my mind is probably that I resent his insisting on the 'privilege' which I once granted him. Funny." That he really deplored snobbishness comes out in *The Pretty Lady* (1918). Hoape is a middle-class man of no special distinction. Yet when he enters a shop to buy boots, he is turned into a "god." So long as workers in shops and factories, whether from choice or coercion, were subservient menials, there was not much prospect for socialism.

Bennett's remarks on millworkers and shopgirls are for the most part concerned with the group or class generically. His views on servants are summarized in the pocket philosophies, but given concrete individuality in the fiction.

---

[13] *Elsie and the Child* (New York: George H. Doran, 1924), p. 328.

He was, of course, acquainted with the numerous portraits of servants in Balzac, Zola, the Goncourts, and others, but his own sketches are not mere imitations. However diverse his servants may be, there is implicit and often explicit a poignant absurdity in their position. Even the rather stolid have a feeble gleam of spirit which defies extinction. But the very relationship of servant to master makes of self-respect an impertinence and of yearning for pleasure a sin.

[In *The Old Wives' Tale* old ways do crumble, and shortly after 1900 a revolution has occurred in the Baines household, but its fruits are really very modest. At the outset Maggie spends "seventeen hours of each day in an underground kitchen and larder, and the other seven in an attic" (9). For Constance she is a "dehumanized drudge," an "organism" (147). Yet on leaving to get married she weeps at giving up so good a home. After years have passed, the new maid, Maud, who occupies the same "cave," has a very different view of her position. In fact, she is an impudent girl, whose motto is "War on employers" (553). But the measure of her revolt is ambiguous; for Sophia, though shaken in her assumptions about the natural order of things, summarily crushes the threat of anarchy and only afterward performs a humane act—not by allowing, but by imperially directing Maud to use the kitchen gas to save her eyes while reading. Thus does Bennett epitomize three decades and more of change, and, moreover, Maud is atypical in her boldness.] Indeed, in 1910 Bennett noted that Marguerite's own French maid rose at six and was never free until nine at night. She seemed "just an ignorant passive slave." When he suggested that the girl go out more often, Marguerite remonstrated that "it would spoil her" (*Journal*, June 6).

Like *The Old Wives' Tale*, the Clayhanger novels start in an earlier time; but one passage in *Hilda Lessways* seems to transcend chronology. Hilda will in time become self-ishly callous about servants, but early in her life she is shocked by the servitude of her mother's pretty young maid scrubbing the kitchen floor:

> She was witnessing now the first stage in the progress of a victim of the business of domesticity. To-day Florrie was a charming young creature, full of slender grace. Soon she would be a dehumanized drudge. And Hilda could not stop it! All over the town, in every street of the town, behind all the nice curtains and blinds, the same hidden shame was being enacted: a vast, sloppy, steaming, greasy, social horror—inevitable! It amounted to bar-barism, Hilda thought in her revolt. (48)

Certainly to use such unrestrained language Bennett must have felt that it was still relevant in 1911. In "The Future" (1908), included in *Paris Nights*, he had protested that the British were enslaving servants, and he suggested that the increased turnover presaged the eventual disappearance of the system.

Later, in *These Twain* (1916), Bennett returned to the matter of the servitude in the Five Towns. Inside the houses one could expect to find "an ignoble race of slatternly imprisoned serfs driven by narrow-minded women who themselves were serfs with the mentality of serfs and the prodigious conceit of virtue" (104). Despite her earlier revulsion, Hilda herself now perceives "no shame" in working her domestics sixteen hours a day (362). The inurement of servants is epitomized in the charwoman, Mrs. Tams, who "lived as naturally in injustice as a fish in water" (383).

Far the most interesting of the fictional servants is Elsie of *Riceyman Steps* (1923), and "Elsie and the Child," (1924). In sketching her history Bennett contrasted her inner sweetness with her sordid surroundings. At first she is living in squalor in the midst of disease and poverty. Later

she and Joe feel fortunate to have employment in a doc-
tor's household, and Elsie enjoys the privacy and domes-
ticity in their cellar abode. Yet, as Bennett describes it,
the room "was actually a cave, subterranean, and felt
like a cave." [14] There has been little change since Florrie
scrubbed the kitchen floor.

One cannot read far in Bennett without discovering a
continuing preoccupation with marriage and with the
unsatisfactory education and position of middle-class
women, whether as daughters or wives. Even his playful
narratives that involve marital conflict and its resolution
support his main theses because their heroines are the
products of the kind of education and cultural traditions
which he deplored. Whatever their intelligence, they have
only trivial outlets for its expression.

The romance of marriage, which appears in a number
of stories, will concern us later. But what of the institution
itself and the home that too often resulted? Marriage
should represent, at its best, an affinity of like minds, and,
as a minimum, a cooperative adventure of two persons
willing to curb their natural egoism for mutual advantage.
The actual consequences of marriage, however, might be
a travesty of its proper intent. In *Whom God Hath Joined*
(1906), the title quickly becomes ironic, for no benign
divinity has shaped the marriage of Lawrence Ridware to
a heartless creature or of Alma Fearns to a philanderer.
Ridware is finally able to break his bonds, but after a
barbaric exposure in the divorce court the Fearnses will
remain legally bound together. In *These Twain* Ingpen's
lunatic wife is "tied up to him just as if she was tied to a
post" (487). These are only the extreme examples of
unhappy marriages held together by law or almost equally
inexorable convention.

More commonly, as in "The British Home," in *Paris*

[14] *Ibid.*, p. 36.

Nights, Bennett was concerned with the fact that women were not educated for their role in marriage and that they willingly acquiesced in a system that could only bring frustration and mental sterility. He once argued that in an arranged marriage in France a girl would have a better chance for success than an English girl who married for love: "She does not imagine that her life is ready made. She knows that she has to build it up." [15] In the same essay, published in 1923, when presumably some liberation of women had occurred, he protested that wives had no genuine interests "outside the narrow sphere of the home" and so no "intellectual independence" (140–141).

Even when a wife or daughter is not the serf of an Ephraim Tellwright, she may be oppressed by custom. In *Leonora* young Rose must battle for her freedom, which she finally achieves by passing a medical examination and going to work in a hospital. At the end of the story her idle class-conscious mother suspects that civilization is wrong and "that Rose and the earnest ones were justified in their scorn of such as her" (341). In the *Clayhanger* trilogy Janet Orgreave is tied with a silken cord, for despite her parents' kindnesses, she is expected to remain at home as eventual nurse and housekeeper. Bennett insists that her sacrifice is typical.

In 1920 he published the book indicatively entitled *Our Women: Chapters on the Sex-Discord.* Writing of the period "just closed," he protested that "in the top class men did not demand any practical expertness whatever" in wives and that there was no "regular educational machinery" for securing it (37). Even worse, a wife's uselessness was necessary "to prove to the world by ocular demonstration that her man had the means to keep a woman in luxury and idleness" (38). Chapter 2 bears the title "The Abolition of Slavery." Among the masters is the father who

[15] "Sex-Rivalry," in *Things That Have Interested Me (Second Series),* p. 136.

"plays the shield and buckler" role for his daughters. In *Things That Have Interested Me (Second Series)* Bennett called segregation of the sexes in university life a "dreadful thing," and he added that "the professed disdainful attitude of undergraduates towards girls was equally deplorable" (7).

If anything, Bennett's concern intensified as time went on. The spoiling of women is central in *The Love Match* (1922). Adela, the wife of Lord Raingo, is without useful occupation. And in novel after novel Bennett managed to use someone as his critical spokesman. Perhaps the most savage outburst enlivens *Mediterranean Scenes* (1928). Speaking of the modernizing of women's customs in Constantinople, he goes on to hope that Turkish women will not imitate the débutante of London and New York, who spends her time dressing, dancing, drinking tea, playing bridge, and again dancing in an "extraordinary routine of fatuousness" (73).

A scarcely less sharp denunciation appears in "Myrtle at 6:a.m.," published in *The Night Visitor*, in 1931. Myrtle is spoiled and idle, but she has the honesty to tell her fiancé that she is a "rotter" and that he should send her to business college. To her inconsequential mother she speaks pure Bennett:

> How am I educated? I can speak French and German, in a way. But what's that? But what can I do? I've been brought up to be idle and spend money and enjoy myself. Only I don't enjoy myself. I hate it all. I only live as I do because I was taught to live like that, and because all the other girls do it. (193)[16]

Balzac and Maupassant, and in England George Moore had depicted frustrated, foot-loose women, and literary

[16] In several light stories in the volume, including "The Night Visitor," the same sentiment is prominent.

tradition, of course, included the *femme fatale*. By the 1920's others besides Bennett were finding a place in novels and the drama for neurotic heroines. Certainly he was influenced by what he read. Again, however, he had his own evidence, and he gave some individuality to his creations.

Cora Ussher in the title story of *The Woman Who Stole Everything* (1927) is a lazy slattern, deceitful, and even brazenly immoral. Her power over men, including her husband, resides in her physical attractiveness and imperious manner. A spiritual cannibal, she is also a lost soul, useless and pathetic. But her loneliness does not make her unique; she is only a symptom of what is wrong with the world in which she finds such tawdry outlets in her search for importance. Bennett calls her "desirable, marvellous and magnificent . . . one of the finished products of a civilization." [17]

Two years later he was driving in Paris with an English woman friend, who wanted a pair of galoshes. When they found a store that sold them, his companion became interested instead in a pair of satin shoes, which, after half an hour, she bought. When reminded of the galoshes, she replied, "Yes, I suppose I may as well get a pair" (*Journal 1929*, 12). The whole affair, to Bennett's amusement—and annoyance—had taken an hour. His note does not elaborate, but clearly he regarded the incident as symptomatic of the boredom and triviality of a woman's existence when she possessed no worthy occupation. Light though it was, it may have served as a touchstone when, at about the same time, Bennett turned to the portrayal of the restless, foot-loose Gracie in *The Imperial Palace*. Gracie, a rich spoiled girl, forced by ennui to resort to cheap thrills, is Bennett's most extended study of frustra-

[17] *The Woman Who Stole Everything* (New York: George H. Doran, 1927), p. 69. The volume consists of reprints from 1924–1927.

tion and confusion of values. Fancying that she is rebelling against the world in which she is an unchallenged conqueror, she indulges in self-revulsion because of her uselessness and makes believe that she would like to be the cash girl in a restaurant. She buys ugly clothing and lives in an unsightly apartment. In her boredom she even seduces Orcham—in the midst of all her squalor. Bennett does not explore her psychology, but cause and effect are clear. Gracie finds a pathological fascination in vulgarity and sensuality because she has been starved emotionally in the world of the traditionally normal. [18]

In *Flora*, acted in 1927, Bennett fused impressions which he had set forth in *Leonora* a generation earlier with views that were at least daring in the England of the late 1920's. Like Leonora, Flora Hammylton is an unhappy, useless wife, but she is less passive. To her husband's amazement, she leaves home and becomes the manager of a dance hall. Finally she gives up Alec Gabriel, rather more a sympathetic friend than a lover, and returns home. Knowing the consequences of unconventional behavior, she has warned her daughter Clare against continuing a liaison with a married man. Indeed, the man himself has done so, too. But when Clare is still determined to accompany her lover to Fontainebleau, Flora encourages her, assuring her that when trouble comes, she can always return to her mother. When working on the play in 1925, Bennett recorded the opinion of a German theatrical friend that "it was a sign of a wholesome public (in England, in contrast to Germany) that such a plot, so simple, should be certain to arouse protest" (*Journal*, July 17). The *Journal* does not say whether the prediction was correct.

Bennett would, of course, have admitted that Gracie

---

[18] The neurasthenic idle rich girl appears also in "Baccarat," in *The Night Visitor*. A slight story, it ends happily only after the girl has lost money she does not possess and has threatened suicide.

and Flora were not typical women of the 1920's. But he would have insisted that they were only heightened symbols of the current social unhealthfulness. Because of custom, women were not greatly freer than Sophia Baines in the 1860's. Their search for identity could lead to revolt that was either fatuous or accompanied by peril.

When Bennett appraised the culture of his time he tended to think of the daily experiences of the "plain man and his wife." What was it like to live in the Five Towns or to be a middle-class citizen of London? The sensation of walking along Cobridge Street and of stopping at the George Hotel was as much a part of one's cultural existence as sitting through a concert at the Albert Hall or wandering in the shadows of cathedrals.

In the Five Towns Bennett's sensations varied from romantic appreciation of the picturesque spectacle to annoyance with details that affronted his eyes. In "The Death of Simon Fuge" (1907), he accepted their "squalid ugliness on a scale so vast and overpowering that it became sublime." [19] But in "England Again" (1907), included in *Paris Nights*, he complained of the "dirt, a public slatternliness, a public and shameless flouting of the virtues of cleanliness and tidiness" (273). In *The Price of Love* (1914), he let Rachel walk along a "frowsy street, whose meanness and monotony of tiny-bow-windows exemplified intensely the most deplorable characteristics of a district where brutish license is [now] decreasing." [20]

In accord with the depressing houses and streets is the grayness of the spirit of the inhabitants. That they work hard would be a virtue for Bennett, except that they are impelled by a mere sense of duty rather than guided by liberating ideals. Rachel conforms to the local mores, but

[19] *Tales of the Five Towns: Including "The Grim Smile of the Five Towns"* (London: Chatto and Windus, 1964), p. 270.
[20] *The Price of Love* (Birmingham: C. Combridge, 1962), p. 271.

through her mildly rebellious thoughts Bennett delimits
the mental horizons of her class:

> She belonged to the middle class . . . which is responsible
> for the Five Towns reputation for joylessness, the class
> which sticks its chin out and gets things done (however
> queer the things done may be), the class which keeps the
> district together and maintains its solidity, the class
> which is ashamed of nothing but idleness, frank enjoy-
> ment, and the caprice of the moment. (Its idiomatic
> phrase for expressing the experience of gladness, "I sang,
> 'O be joyful,'" alone demonstrates its unwillingness to
> rejoice.) (190)

Rachel has been attracted by the hedonism of the irresponsible Louis, and now she finds that even he seems to
say: "The fun is over. We must be strictly conventional
now" (190).

In *The Old Wives' Tale* Bennett calls the Five Towns
medieval and notes that they had no free libraries or
municipal parks. In *Clayhanger* he speaks of their "perhaps
excessive provincialism" (3). And in *The Savour of Life*
(1928), he complains of a pervading narrowness in "the
provinces."[21] Even the manners of the people were
grudging and reserved, as if expression of feeling, especially among relatives, were improper. For that matter, in
Mr. Prohack Lady Mussulman, who likes the English,
protests that as a nation "they give themselves never!
They are shut like their lips over their long teeth" (204).

In London Bennett found the same lack of fun, the
same joylessness, as in the Five Towns. Audrey in *The
Lion's Share* (1916) asks what Londoners do "when they
want to be jolly." Miss Ingate replies: "They never want
to be jolly. . . . If they feel as if they couldn't help being

[21] *The Savour of Life: Essays in Gusto* (New York: Doubleday, Doran and
Co., 1928), p. 21. The volume consists of reprinted articles.

jolly, then they hire a private room somewhere and draw the blinds down" (156). Ten years earlier, in *Whom God Hath Joined*, Bennett had spoken of London as being filled with people bustling aimlessly "who must inevitably die before they had begun to live, and to whom the possession of their souls in contemplation would always be an impossibility" (285). In *The Roll Call* he paralleled Rachel's sensations of the dismal Five Towns street. George Cannon is walking through what is a quite respectable quarter of London. Through the windows of the areaways he sees "the furtive existence of squalor behind barred windows,"

> and as he raised his eyes to the drawing-room and bedroom stories he found no relief. His eyes could discover nothing that was not mean, ugly, frowzy, and unimaginative . . . . The city worked six days in order to be presented with this on the seventh. Truly it was very similar to the Five Towns, and in essentials not a bit better. (59)

For many persons in the provinces the only relief was standardized amusement (*Roll Call*, 241), and for the London physician, Dr. Cashmore, of *Buried Alive* (1908), there was nothing "more paradisaical than a Sunday Pullman escapade to Brighton" (18). As for what one found at Brighton—or at any other seacoast resort—Bennett recorded Clayhanger's impressions:

> The self-satisfied gestures of men inspecting their cigars or lifting glasses, of simpering women glancing on the sly at their jewels, and of youths pulling straight their white waistcoats as they strolled about with the air of Don Juans, invigorated his contempt for the average existence. (*Clayhanger*, 491) [22]

[22] Bennett was at least as severe on American culture. Besides his repeated strictures in *Your United States*, he wrote Hugh Walpole in December, 1919, that he could not "stick" the "plutocratic society" in New York (*Letters of Arnold Bennett*, Vol. III, *1916–1931*, ed. James Hepburn [London: Oxford University Press, 1970], p. 116).

For Bennett, who enjoyed physical comforts, the traditional indifference to them amounted to cultural backwardness. When Clayhanger installs a gas stove and other
amenities in his bedroom and is twitted by his friends for
being a sybarite, his reflections on the matter are clearly
Bennett's own:

> The average bedroom of the average English household
> was so barbaric that during eight months of the year you
> could not maintain your temperature in it unless you
> were either in your bed or running about the room,
> and . . . even in summer you could not sit down therein
> at ease because there was nothing to sit on, nor a table
> to sit at, nor even a book to read. (*These Twain*, 14–15)

Mr. Prohack is a winsome man, but also a comic one,
whose attempts to be an individual are often unimaginatively conventional. His home, just behind Hyde Park
Gardens, is meant to be typical of upper-middle-class
opulence:

> The dining room, simply finished with reproductions of
> chaste Chippendale, and chilled to the uncomfortable
> low temperature that hardy Britons pretend to enjoy,
> formed part of an unassailable correct house of mid-
> Victorian style and antiquity . . . . (9)

Clayhanger lives in a transitional period, but Mr. Prohack
is well within the twentieth century.

Hotels and clubs were also, for Bennett, indications of
the amenities of a civilization. He considered himself an
authority both on luxury city hotels and on their staid
provincial counterparts. In *The Regent* (1913) he humor-
ously sketched one of the latter, a very respectable
institution:

> And in justice to the Turk's Head it is to be clearly stated
> that it did no more to cow and discourage travelers than

any other provincial hotel in England. It was a sound and serious English provincial hotel, and it linked century to century.[23]

In *The Roll Call* Cannon once eats "the customary desolating table-d'hôte dinner which is served simultaneously in the vast, odorous dining rooms, all furnished alike, of scores and scores of grand hotels throughout the provinces" (240).

Bennett repeatedly turned into amusement his irritation with clubs: intended to serve a member's convenience and put him at ease, they intimidated and disheartened. The one in which Priam Farll is a guest, in *Buried Alive*, resembles a "town hall": "In gigantic basins chiselled out of solid granite, Priam scrubbed his finger-nails with a nail brush larger than he had previously encountered, even in nightmares . . ." (141). In *The Roll Call* Cannon "soon reached the stage at which a club member asserts gloomily that the club cookery is simply damnable" (117). And Mr. Prohack finally "decided that the club was a dreary haunt, and could not understand why he had never before perceived its dreariness" (272).

In all his strictures on contemporary society Bennett was, of course, dependent on fragmentary impressions, and he spoke with much less assurance of London than of the Five Towns. For some things he certainly drew upon the newspapers and upon current books, and probably also upon remarks by such friends as H. G. Wells. Whatever his sources, his perspective is that of a man who wants the mechanics of industrial and social life to be efficient and is distressed by ineptness, who wants freedom for individual creativity and finds indifference or suppression, who wants an atmosphere of gracious ease and urbanity and confronts uncouthness and infelicities.

[23] *The Regent: A Five-Towns Story of Adventure in London* (London: Methuen and Co., 1965), p. 42.

Naturally, Bennett was specially concerned with popular literary and artistic taste. Besides the oblique references in his literary criticism, there are a number of pointed attacks on the reading public. In *Whom God Hath Joined* we find the gratuitous phrase, "the demand for books in the Five Towns being inferior to any other demand whatsoever" (66). In "England Again" (in *Paris Nights*), we read that although drunkenness in the Five Towns has decreased, "we possess 750 licensed houses and not a single proper bookshop" (272). The sharpest diatribe is in the essay "The Novel-Reading Public" (1909), where Bennett laments that no really good novelist can please the novel-buying middle class on which his livelihood depends, and this because "the dullest class in England takes to novels merely as a refuge from its own dullness." [24] In *Things That Have Interested Me (Second Series)* there is again much on the vapidity of current popular books. Here Bennett is not altogether consistent, since he himself was not always willing to yield to a difficult book the time it deserved, and since his own fantasias were mere entertainment. But his main charge was against the popular predilection for books that were tastelessly sentimental and devoid of sensitivity of style. Such a complaint could have been justified only against the slightest of his own works.

When we turn to Bennett's comments on the fine arts we are faced with the question of his competence for judging. He was interested in the subject matter of a painting or statue and he wanted a vitality that would give immediate emotional excitement. As we have noticed, in the Greek statue of the woman he at once sensed a story—the relation of a man and a maid. In this, of course, there is nothing wrong; indeed it may be good. But it is no indication of subtlety in artistic appreciation. What we can be sure of, however, is Bennett's honesty. His protests were

[24] Hynes, *The Author's Craft*, p. 82.

against indifference to the arts and, even more, against
snobbishness and hypocrisy.

In *What the Public Wants* (1909) Sir Charles Worgan is
an influential publisher of newspapers and journals who,
as the title implies, provides the reading market with what
it wants, and is himself the epitome of public crassness. A
theatrical manager chides him, "You're afraid of beauty;
you detest originality; and as for truth, it makes you hold
your nose."[25] In *Buried Alive* and *The Great Adventure*, its
dramatic version, the art buying public is equally rich
and inane, and it is the name of Priam Farll, not the merits
of his painting, that sets its prices. In *From the Log of the
Velsa* (1914), Bennett remarks that "the majority and
backbone of the world have not yet begun to be artistically
civilized" (95). The complaints continue into the 1920's.
During and just after the war Bennett waxed especially
vehement concerning what he once called "female
artistic snobs," who perverted bazaars into fatuous social
affairs.[26]

Bennett's scattered comments on architecture attack
primarily the meanness in the proportions of buildings and
the meretricious debasement of ornamental detail. An
example of meanness is the newspaper building in "The
Matador of the Five Towns," which is "capacious and
considerable, but horribly faced with terra cotta, and quite
unimposing, lacking in the spectacular effect; like nearly
everything in the Five Towns, carelessly and scornfully
ugly."[27] As for the meretricious, Bennett, not surprisingly,
found it most strikingly in the upper part of the Albert
Memorial, which in *The Glimpse* he damned as "an im-
moderate unsightliness" (237).

[25] *What the Public Wants: A Play in Four Acts* (New York: George H. Doran, 1909), p. 71.

[26] Letter to Mrs. Elsie Herzog, September 7, 1918 (*Letters*, III, 68).

[27] *The Matador of the Five Towns* (Birmingham: C. Combridge, 1963), pp. 6–7.

Bennett's most ambitious venture into architectural criticism occurs in *The Roll Call*, where his hero is an architect. There he accuses Vanbrugh of ruining the Royal hospital with "corrupt brick and flaming manifestations of decadence" which are "an outrage upon Jones and Wrenn" (141). Indeed, Bennett was interested both in form as conceived by the architect and in the emotional impression of the viewer. Some seventeen years earlier he had praised the new Roman Catholic cathedral, then under construction, for "asserting itself so mildly yet so irresistibly amid the heaped-up ugliness of the West End, a superb refutation of the theory that an inartistic age can produce nothing artistic." [28] In "A Chamber Concert" he again damned the typical architecture while praising the exception—this time the Central Hall at Westminster, which was the only concert hall not "architecturally offensive" (*Things, Second Series*, 185).

Bennett was intensely fond of music, and in "The Death of Simon Fuge" he gives a delightful picture of two amateur enthusiasts who play duets after their day's work is over. What he could not endure was the turning of music into a cultural artifact. The typical performance in a concert hall—in contrast to that in music halls—killed the spirit of a work by the very unnaturalness of the occasion. Writing of one concert, Bennett even disparaged the appearance of the audience, which "consisted in the main of ugly Calvinistic, peculiar or superior people." He continued, "Why are the frequenters of serious concerts so alarmingly ugly, and why do their features usually denote harsh intellectuality and repudiation?" (*ibid.*, 185–186). A concert was too often a ritual to be endured. [29]

Despite his enthusiastic language about music even at a

[28] "The Fallow Fields of Fiction," in Hynes, *The Author's Craft*, p. 66.
[29] In *The Lion's Share* a spokesman for Bennett accuses the London musical public of unimaginatively depending "absolutely on Germany" (364).

concert, as a source of inspiration in *The Book of Carlotta*, Bennett could not fully divorce it from the milieu in which it was played, and, as with art, he was inclined to look for the story in it—a story in which the listeners were often the principal interest. Hence, in theory at least, he could justify the music halls. Thus in "The Hanbridge Empire" (in *Paris Nights*), he wrote: "Even the newspaper-lad and the match-girl might go to the Hanbridge Empire and, sitting together, drink the milk of paradise. Wonderful discoverers, these new music-hall directors all up and down the United Kingdom. They have discovered the folk" (279). One senses in the numerous laments about concert-goers an undue eagerness to detect snobbishness and insincerity. But, once again, there is an honest insistence that art must excite the imagination and intensify one's sensation of being alive.

When discussing the theater, Bennett wrote as a practicing playwright. Eventually he was to submit two especially ambitious plays, *Don Juan de Marana* (completed in 1914, published in 1923) and *Judith* (1919). In several of his others he unmistakably tried to give the public what it wanted—a mild conflict of wills, with some gentle scolding of society, a few exhortations in the manner of the pocket philosophies, and a pleasant reconciliation at the curtain. Indeed, his strictures on the theatrical taste of his compatriots might well apply to his own audiences. Having converted *Anna of the Five Towns* into *Cupid and Commonsense*, with the original somber ending giving way to a contrived comic one, Bennett included in the published version (1908) a preface "on the Crisis in the Theatre." In it he spoke of the new theaters being built "in response to the demand of untrained, child-like intelligences just arousing themselves to the significance of things." [30]

[30] *Cupid and Commonsense: A Play in Four Acts* (New York: George H. Doran, n.d.), p. 22.

The following year, in *What the Public Wants*, a character makes merry with the stereotypes of the London stage, among them the clever, whimsical widow and the "wise, gentle, cunning, well-dressed philosopher of fifty" (134–135). Bennett himself, to be sure, created both whimsical women and philosophic gentlemen. Quite another kind of characters and plot is alluded to in *Clayhanger*, where Snaggs's popular Five-Towns theater, once known as the "Blood Tub," has specialized in "melodrama and murder and gore" (301). Concerning the theatrical world Bennett invariably wrote as a disillusioned insider. An epitome of his feeling is an entirely gratuitous reference in "Honour," one of the stories in *The Night Visitor*, to "the entire, withdrawn, self-centred, aspiring, infinitely tedious, self-deceiving world of the theatre" (125). And in the unfinished *Dream of Destiny* we read: "What a frightful career the stage! She was an authentic star, but she was not exempt from the disasters inseparable from the career." [31]

Nowhere in Bennett is there any systematic discussion of the theory of drama, nor is there evidence of his serious study of great tragedies. Since the plays of which he was single or coauthor are not passionate, soul-shaking affairs, it is impossible to know just how he would have defined a play worthy of a mature audience. We can say, however, that, though he was not entirely guiltless of either sin, he deplored sentimentality and the artificial trappings of sophistication. The theater too often served up easy solutions to human predicaments and resorted to smartness to disguise its paucity of substance. In short, it was dull. So it is that, after complaining of the standardization of entertainment "throughout the provinces," Bennett, in *The Roll Call*, has Cannon laugh at "the inventive drollery of the knock-about comedians—Britain's sole genuine con-

[31] *Dream of Destiny, an Unfinished Novel, and Venus Rising from the Sea* (London: Cassell, 1932), p. 185.

tribution to the art of the modern stage" (241). As in the
music hall, there might be uncouthness here, but there
was also vitality.

October 24, 1926, Bennett went walking in the late
morning sunshine. Suddenly any pleasant thoughts he
may have had were annihilated when he heard a congregation singing. In his *Journal* he wrote simply, "I visu-
alized the inside of the conventicle and hated the thought
of my youth." His bitterness had not abated since he had
let it guide his pen in *Anna of the Five Towns* (1902). Indeed,
of all aspects of the culture of his time the practice of
religion was for Bennett the worst. To what extent his own
habits of rigid, sometimes arbitrary, self-discipline may
have been influenced by the severity of the Methodist
civilization in which he was reared is, of course, con-
jectural. In any event, Methodism as Bennett experienced
it meant the belief that man was a fallen creature who
should persistently tread a narrow road toward redemp-
tion, and for whom the only true joy would come from a
feeling that he was on the way toward it. Hence it represented a spirit of gloom varied only by protestation—
commonly public—of the blessedness of conversion. For
Bennett the gloom was a needless and superstitious
affliction and the public admission of one's past sins and
his dedication to virtue was prideful and mawkish. The
Primitive Methodism was, of course, the most oppressive
kind. It was not really the doctrine that concerned
Bennett. Rather it was the mood—the tenor of life. In fact,
it would appear that a spirit of self-denial and fear of
enjoyment was indigenous to the Five Towns, since some
of Bennett's characters who are not religious at all are
zealous abstainers from pleasure. Religious practices were
merely its most public expression. To the Ten Command-
ments too many of the citizens had added an eleventh,
Thou shalt neither enjoy nor encourage enjoyment.

In *Things That Have Interested Me: Third Series*, published in the same year as his *Journal* comment, Bennett
entitled one section "Passing of the Puritans." Crediting
the Victorian Puritan spirit with giving "strength of mind
and the ability cheerfully to 'do without,'" he continued,
however, "It was the enemy of pleasure.... Naturally
it developed narrow-mindedness, bigotry, hypocrisy, and
spiritual conceit" (199). In the section "My Religious
Experience" he retold how his father, who had virtually
ceased to attend church, made sure that the children
suffered:

> Sunday was the worst day of the week, anticipated with
> horror, and finished with an exquisite relief. Two
> attendances at Sunday school and two religious services
> in a day! About six hours in durance.... It was
> inevitable that religion should come to be unalterably
> connected in my mind with the ideas of boredom,
> injustice, and insincerity. (213)

In *Anna of the Five Towns* (1902) Ephraim Tellwright is
said to have been "what is termed 'a good Wesleyan,'
preaching and teaching, and spending himself in the
various activities of Hanbridge chapel." [32] Bennett finds it
in no way strange that in his later years Ephraim is a
self-righteous, relentless, miserly tyrant. Titus Price, the
tragic victim of Ephraim's financial heartlessness, is both
a Sunday school superintendent and a hypocrite. Bennett
respected the two men enough to make Tellwright a major
figure and to secure pity for Titus. The revivalist, who
appears briefly, was, on the contrary, an affront to his
sensibilities: "I have been called a mountebank," he
rants; "I am one. I glory in it. I am God's mountebank,
doing God's business in my own way" (73). Even the
generous Mrs. Sutton is contaminated. Her innate good-

[32] *Anna of the Five Towns: A Novel* (New York: George H. Doran, 1915),
p. 23.

ness prevents her doing serious mischief; but in her naïve, conventional faith she makes Anna feel that in refusing to accept the revivalist's invitation to ready-made salvation she is "proud, stiff-necked, obstinate in iniquity" (80). The shame which Anna endures is degrading. Far from being purified by her anguished soul-searching, she must recover from her humiliation as from a disease. If Ephraim represents a traducing of Old Testament ideals, the revivalist and his disciples are a profanation of the New.

In *Leonora*, published the next year, William Twenlow is characterized as one "in whom an unbridled appetite for virtue becomes a vice" (40). Bennett shows him no mercy: "He loved God with such virulence that he killed his wife, drove his daughter into a fatuous marriage, and quarreled with his son" (40). Old Meschach is something of a card, but in exposing John Stanway's fraud he is moved "partly by an almost biblical sense of justice, a sense blind, callous, cruel" (58). Leonora herself has been constrained by hypocritical traditions, and she is married to a hypocrite, whose answer to his daughters has always been "no." She envisions a home where parents and children can be natural, "instead of like the virtuous and the martyrized puppets of a terrible system called 'acting for the best'" (183).

Between 1908 and 1916 Bennett was especially preoccupied with his revulsion against organized religion. In "The Matador of the Five Towns," written in 1908, he wanted to present the tragic misfortune of his hero in an indifferent society, and he could not resist attacking the spiritual emptiness and hypocrisy of the churchgoing community. The children come out of a "dark brown Sunday school" to enter an equally "dark brown chapel"; the clanging temple bells announce the "different gods of the Five Towns"; and dapper priests and acolytes hurry along, "the convinced heralds of eternal salvation" (39).

The very first page of *The Old Wives' Tale*, published in the same year, refers to the "religious orgies" practiced a little north of Bursley, presumably by the Primitive Methodists. In chapter 5 Bennett returns to the Methodists, alluding to the Primitive sect, with its chapel on King Street, and to the Wesleyans at Duck Bank. The tone is of sheer merriment. Jehovah is a "God of sixty or so with a mustache and beard," and Satan is "an obscene monstrosity, with cloven hoofs and a tail, very dangerous and rude" (93). The time is when Sophia and Constance were still young, and the congregation is large. At the time he is writing, Bennett indicates, it would be sparse. Presumably by then, too, God and Satan would be less comic. Still, in the next year, in *What the Public Wants*, a character remarks that in any London play "you've only got to mention the word Methodist, and the whole house will go into fits" (113). He suggests that a tragic play should concern the Church of England: "That will at least make people gloomy" (123).

The most sustained and diverse portrayal of religious excess and hypocrisy is in the *Clayhanger* trilogy. The substance is not autobiography, but, as Edwin grows to manhood in the Five Towns, it was easy for Bennett to include his own personal impressions. In the first of the three parts, Darius Clayhanger, like Ephraim Tellwright, is a creature of Puritanism, not so much by creed as in attitude. But the new, energetic minister, who adds Saturday afternoon Bible class to the Sunday afternoon Sunday school, represents the most repellent form of missionary zeal: "It was gross tyranny and nothing else" (57). Bennett's comment in his *Journal* in 1926 merely rephrases the feelings he attributes to Edwin, who in retrospect hates Sunday schools: "They were connected in his memory with atrocious tedium, pietistic insincerity, and humiliating contacts" (224). At the centenary of Sunday schools

Edwin feels revulsion at the people's primitive "gloating over inexhaustible tides of blood . . . . It seemed to him that the drums were tom-toms and Baines's a bazaar" (244). Edwin is ambivalent about the vicar of St. Peter's, but at least the vicar is no mountebank: "He never, with a shamed, defiant air, said, 'I am not ashamed of Christ,' like the Wesleyans" (384). The time is 1887.

In *Hilda Lessways* Bennett returns to the Primitive Methodists, living to the north of the Five Towns in villages "whose red-flaming furnaces illustrated the eternal damnation which was the chief article of their devout religious belief" (29). *These Twain* restates Edwin's bitterness about Sunday schools; and in mock heroic approval of the hypocrite Albert Benbow, Bennett writes: "He was a happy man. In early adolescence he had taken to Sunday Schools as some youths take to vice" (114).

Like Ephraim and Darius, Auntie Hamps is too intriguing to be summed up in a caricature. Her hypocrisy is so ingenious and so nicely sustained that it becomes romantic. But she is, of course, an illustration of the fatuousness of conventional moral and religious codes. On her squalid deathbed she is scandalized by the pregnancy of her servant and insists on her dismissal. Her burial epitomizes the inconsistency in hypocrisy itself. Before the service begins, the avaricious auntie is, for those gathered about, "the paragon of all excellence." Then the three ministers take over and, with equal disregard for the actual Auntie Hamps, make use of her as a typical subject for Christian ritual; and so she is suddenly once again transformed, this time into "a sinner snatched from the consequences of sin by a miracle of divine sacrifice" (446).

Hypocrisy was also found, of course, quite apart from religious observances. In *Books and Persons*, consisting of articles written in 1909–1911, Bennett repeatedly attacked the middle class for sentimental evasion of reality. His

protests continued into the twenties. By comparison, the
new age was superior to that of his childhood and youth.
In an essay "Dancing," included in *Things That Have
Interested Me* (*Second Series*) (1923), he found an excuse to
sum up his feelings:

> I am willing to admit that the Victorian Age was a great
> age, though it acutely exasperated me when I was young.
> But that it had the terrible vices of continual repression
> and disgusting hypocrisy cannot be disputed, and to
> contemplate its corpse gives me genuine pleasure. (110)

Nevertheless, in the third series of *Things That Have
Interested Me* (1926), Bennett inveighed against new reform
societies concerned with "meddling with other people's
beliefs and conduct which are perhaps the second greatest
curse of existence in Great Britain" (196). The change
was, apparently, after all, a modest one.

In reviewing Bennett's strictures upon late Victorian
and early twentieth-century life we have, of course, been
limiting ourselves to the views of a man who had had some
unpleasant experiences and who, in the exercise of his
profession, was naturally at times a gadfly. What is of
interest, however, is that we have not been dealing with
some theoretician who might take a lofty view and regret
that the generality of mankind were not equally wise, nor
have we been concerned with a splenetic censor, a self-
appointed village scold. Instead, we have looked through
the eyes of an intelligent man very much immersed in the
activities of the world, but trying to achieve enough
detachment to cast out the waste and the dross.

Whether delivered with serious warmth or suggested
playfully in a comedy or fantasia, there is in Bennett's
work the recurrent theme that men go after the wrong
things. They want success, but do not have any notion of
what it should be. Bennett's own standards are not un-

realistic. One simple and obvious measure, as he remarked in the *Journal*, was the raising of the material standard of living. For himself this might include having a yacht; for anyone it should mean escape from unnecessary discomforts. The incongruity was that people needlessly denied themselves the amenities.

More important was self-respect, for which too often was substituted self-deception. There is nothing wrong with the fact that the inhabitants of Trafalgar Road, in *These Twain*, are proud of their homes. But what is comic is that their naïve snobbishness is based on so absurd a justification: "Conservative or Liberal, they were anti-democratic, even murmuring to themselves as they descended the front steps in the morning and mounted them in the evening: 'Most folks are nobodies, but I am somebody.' And this was true" (4–5). And, of course, self-respect was confused with respectability, and so the path led to hypocrisy as one pretended to be what he took no pleasure in being.

Despite attempts by such persons as Sophia Baines and Edwin Clayhanger to revolt, traditional values continued to prevail. The conventional was fenced in with secure walls and it offered safety. Of course, the walls were always being assaulted, and so one found himself using much of his spiritual energy merely to defend them, with no thought as to what they enclosed. Even in Paris Sophia cannot escape from the traditions of St. Luke's Square. And Edwin is never allowed to forget that he is the son of Darius and of the Five Towns. He sometimes fights for new values as if he understood them, and yet they are illusory.

What do the characters settle for? Anna Tellwright will have an honest, capable husband and a respectable position. She will remain ill at ease in her conscience about her treatment of Titus Price and his son Willie, who has loved her. Her house will always be in order; she will do her share of good works; she will grow old. She has rejected the one precarious adventure which has been offered her, and no new opportunity is likely to occur. Her life will run on, in time downward, and, while noble in its integrity, it will be spiritually uneventful. This is not to say that her life or that of Rachel, in *The Price of Love*, who must look after a husband who is a thief, or Sophia's sojourn in Paris and her return to Bursley is without romance. On the contrary, as we shall notice later, it is substance for Bennett as a romantic novelist. It is rather that the pathos of unfulfillment or at best illusory success for these heroines, for Edwin and Hilda, and even for the genial Mr. Prohack stems from a confusion in values in the society which gives them strength and imprisons them.

The world in which they move is morally and culturally a Ptolemaic one. There is no single principle to give it coherence and consistency; only by tinkering can one make its cosmology seem to work. If many a person is virtuous, if he performs useful deeds, he is still wandering about on a dust-clouded plain rather than standing in the clear atmosphere of a mountain top. He has no perspective from which to look upon his burdensome chores and find purpose or meaning in performing them. Worst of all, he has no sense of the excitement that— in a world not fettered by convention and tradition—can spring from even a modest imaginative creativity.

What can the characters achieve? Only for moments do they have an Aurelian peace of mind. They do best when aroused to action. Lord Raingo is not a better—or worse— philosopher for joining the cabinet; he *is* much more alive. George Cannon is bewildered by military service, which in some ways is senseless; but his ingenuity and determination are tested, and in his physical exhaustion he feels good. The best part of Edwin Clayhanger's life is spent

in hard work and the making of minor industrial improve-
ments. Sophia creates a spotless, efficient, highly respectable boarding house. It would, of course, be better if it
were a delightful homelike place to live in, instead of a
sterile, forbidding establishment. Hilda and other wives
settle for making their presences felt by their husbands
and perhaps by their community. The excitement of
intrigue and contest of wills gives a little zest to their
existence. In general, however, being only housewives,
untrained for their tasks, and having ignoble tools with
which to work and vanity often as their goal, they fare
the worst of the lot. It is not that they are unhappy, but
that their rewards are so small.

If one were to think in the metaphor of a Dantean or
Miltonic myth, without so grim a view of the nether
regions, he could say that Bennett's characters have no
clear glimpse of Paradise or Eden, and that in the confinement of their perspective he felt that they typified
civilization as he knew it. Too often they seem blown about
on the winds like Paolo or Francesca, or, like the fallen
angels, they employ some ingenuity to make Hell en-
durable, but with no thought of escape or even of an imaginative renovation of their quarters. Their Hell is seldom
an acutely painful one. It lacks utter horror except for
moments, and its light is more than darkness visible. Yet,
except when a glint of romance comes into it—and
Bennett tried to cast a number of rays into its purlieus—it
tends toward a grayness, even a mild darkness. Such was
his assessment of his times.

CHAPTER THREE

Adventures Often among Masterpieces

The Truth about an Author (1903) and *How to Become an Author*, of the same year, were by a writer who had only two serious novels to his credit. The two lighthearted treatises dealt in an elementary way with fiction as a craft, and, though they did stress the importance of inspiration for serious work, they had little to say on the subtleties of literary art. By 1931 Bennett was to speak a good deal more about fiction as a fine art, and yet he was never to relinquish his interest in the mere storytelling craft.[1] He was also never to develop a coherent body of literary theory. Consequently, one must not look to find in his comments on literature anything approaching the aesthetic structure created in the prefaces of Henry James or the passionate wrestling with the purposes of fiction that characterizes the prefaces and essays of Joseph Conrad. Nor, as we shall see, was Bennett solidly grounded

[1] As Samuel Hynes remarks, "He brought to his work, and to his judgments of other men's works, two kinds of standards: the standards of the craftsman . . . and the standards of the artist, who aspires to create a permanent and living work of the imagination . . ." (*The Author's Craft*, p. xii).

in the history of literary theory from Aristotle to the 1920's.

What, then, is the value of following him as he roams discursively among novels from the time of Richardson to the days of Sinclair Lewis and Dreiser? The interest is partly, of course, because he admitted that he could not have written as he did except for his debt to certain predecessors. It is even more in the fact that his comments represent a view of literature which, despite its limitations, is sane and useful. He could be delightfully inconsistent, as in his remarks on Richardson, and stubbornly antiaesthetic, as in his underrating of James and Proust. And whether he really read novels as fast as he glibly asserted in *The Truth about an Author* and again in "The Born Reviewer"[2] (1930), he certainly did not choose to give his attention for long at a time to any single work. He was, indeed, very much the plain man who happened to like to read books. But as such he had a healthy, humanistic approach to literature.[3] He always started with life itself as he knew it or believed it to be. A novel had to concern itself with his daily living; he had to need it. Only after he had devoured it, possibly, to be sure, with imperfect digestion, was he willing to consider it as a work of art. And he rightly judged his taste to be sensitive, but not in the remotest degree fastidious. In essence, literature was, first of all, the major province of the humanities. It was also, of course, a fine art.

At the age of twenty-nine Bennett jotted down in his *Journal*, October 15, 1896, a long list of omissions in his knowledge of English literature. He knew little Shakespeare and much less of the great Victorians, including Thomas Hardy. In short, in spite of his avid reading, he

---

[2] *Ibid.*, pp. 266–273.

[3] In 1931 Rebecca West wrote with good-humored exaggeration, "He had no standards of criticism." Yet she liked his critical attacks on contemporaries for their "vein of rich comedy" (*Arnold Bennett Himself*, p. 20).

had been totally unsystematic. On the other hand, he knew well Maupassant and the Goncourts. Moreover, he had acquired a rather large library and had begun wading through much miscellaneous literature. As the decades continued he read more Shakespeare, George Eliot, Meredith, and especially Hardy, became well acquainted with a number of other eighteenth- and nineteenth-century English authors, and immersed himself in the other French realists and in George Moore. He continued to admire Turgenev, and in time he became enthusiastic about Dostoevsky. Never interested in becoming a sound literary scholar, he simply followed his instinct. But while doing so he was concerned with sorting out the first rate from the second and that, in turn, from the third.

Over the years Bennett prepared short lists of great authors for his readers.[4] One such list, of 1904, names Richardson, Scott, Balzac, Stendhal, Turgenev, Flaubert, and Tolstoy.[5] Later he contradicted himself on the importance of Scott and Flaubert; and after repeatedly praising Richardson as a great realist, he finally admitted in 1927 that he was "75 per cent. boring" and that no one had time to read *Clarissa Harlowe*.[6] He would also come to put Dostoevsky above Tolstoy. Other lists include such moderns as Conrad, France, and Dreiser.

Bennett also enjoyed making the most of impulsive enthusiasms. Thus, in 1904, in the somewhat patronizing essay "My Literary Heresies," in which he praised Wordsworth, disparaged Tennyson, and suggested that Browning could not write—views of Tennyson and Browning to be contradicted later—he burst forth in praise of Crashaw's conceits. A few years later, in *Literary Taste:*

---

[4] For example, in *How to Become an Author: A Practical Guide* (London: The Literary Correspondence College, n.d.), pp. 139 ff.

[5] "My Literary Heresies," in Hynes, *The Author's Craft*, p. 237.

[6] "On Re-reading the English Novelists," in *ibid.*, p. 255.

How to Form It, he called Crashaw one of the "narrower geniuses" (27). And in *Clayhanger* and *Hilda Lessways,* despite the fact that the ill-educated Hilda reads Charlotte Yonge, Mrs. Ward, and Mrs. Craik, she also owns Crashaw. Bennett was perhaps a bit eccentric, too, in singling out Wordsworth's *Excursion* for special acclaim in "The Death of Simon Fuge." For a short while, in 1903–1904, as his *Journal* reveals, he was uncommonly interested in the works of Anatole France. In 1913 he called *War and Peace* "tame," though possessed of "extremely beautiful" descriptions (*Journal,* April 7). Then, in 1921, in contrast, he praised *The Death of Ivan Ilyitch,* "than which no story can be better."[7] There were a good many twentieth-century novels which Bennett extolled, even though his interest in them was casual or transitory. Thus, upon reading *Lady Chatterley's Lover* in 1928, he called Lawrence "the most original novelist now writing, except James Joyce" (*Journal,* August 16). Shortly afterward he had to qualify his admiration by objecting to Lawrence's "obsession with the everlasting clash between man and woman."[8]

If Bennett's distribution of accolades seems now and then whimsical, if he blows now hot, now cold, on major novelists and poets, it is because he was not making use of formal criteria for evaluating literary merit, but was recording his immediate response. When Tennyson or Tolstoy did not provide for his emotional and intellectual needs of the moment, he would not give lip service to their greatness.

Yet he was not a mere idle rambler. From the first he was aware of a tension between that view of life and literature which is loosely and ambiguously termed romantic and those views which perhaps even more ambiguously

---

[7] *Things That Have Interested Me,* p. 209.
[8] "The Progress of the Novel" (1929), in Hynes, *The Author's Craft,* p. 96.

are called realistic or naturalistic. As he looked at Burslem under its pall of smoke, he could wax romantic and write in eloquent periodic sentences of its picturesqueness; and as he thought of Sophia Baines and Edwin Clayhanger, he could willingly place in their hearts romantic dreams and ideals which his own heart wished them to have. But he was intrigued also by the circumstantial evidence in life, and as a craftsman he found it absorbing to fit together a structure of realistic detail. In support of his romantic leanings he could go to many an earlier nineteenth-century poet or novelist. For realism, as he himself stated, he turned mainly to France. In fact, in a letter to Miss Lucie Simpson, June 18, 1903, he spoke of *Anna of the Five Towns* as "written of course under French influence throughout." [9]

Yet about three years before *Anna* was published Bennett indicated that he had swung markedly back from an earlier addiction to naturalism. In his *Journal*, January 3, 1899, he wrote that Burne-Jones's "preoccupation with the spiritual, to the ignoring of everyday facts, served to complete in me a modification of view which has been proceeding now for a year or two." He continued:

The day of my enthusiasm for "realism," for "naturalism," has passed. I can perceive that a modern work of fiction dealing with modern life may ignore realism and yet be great. To find beauty, which is always hidden—that is the aim. If beauty is found, then superficial facts are of small importance. But they are of *some* importance. And though I concede that in the past I have attached too high a value to realism, nevertheless I see no reason why it should be dispensed with. My desire is to depict the deeper beauty while abiding by the envelope of facts. At the worst, the facts should not be ignored. They might, for the sake of more clearly disclosing the beauty, suffer a certain *distortion*—I can't think of a better word. Indeed they cannot be ignored in the future. The achievements of the finest French writers, with Turgenev and Tolstoy, have set a standard for all coming masters of fiction.

This would seem to favor romanticism. Yet when Bennett was most in error in judging a work of fiction, he erred because he expected from it a kind of realism which it lacked—something akin to what he found in the French or the Russians. Thus, in 1904, he complained that *Wuthering Heights* would have been much better "if Emily had known about forty times as much as she did concerning life and her trade." [10] In the same essay he granted artistic perfection to *Persuasion;* but in 1927, in "On Re-reading the English Novelists," he protested that Jane Austen's "world is a tiny world, and even of that tiny world she ignores, consciously or unconsciously, the fundamental factors." [11] By now his opinion of George Eliot had risen, essentially because of those aspects of her work that he felt were most realistic. And of Trollope he wrote that, although he had "neither genius nor style," he was nevertheless "a worker and a realist and a non-sentimentalist, and he knew what life is." [12]

Again in 1927, in "The Novels of Eden Phillpotts," Bennett dwelt on the realistic authenticity of the Dartmoor cycle, in which Phillpotts, as a realist, had made his characters "part of his scenery and the scenery . . . part of the characters." Generalizing, he wrote, "In fiction, as in all literature, what most matters is the author's attitude towards the mystery of the universe." Phillpotts's was "scientific so far as science can go. Beyond that it is strictly agnostic." [13] In short, the instinct that initially led

---

[10] "My Literary Heresies," in Hynes, *The Author's Craft*, p. 237.

[11] *Ibid.*, p. 256.

[12] *Ibid.*, p. 262.

[13] *Ibid.*, pp. 172, 178.

Bennett toward the nineteenth-century French novelists and Turgenev, and then on to Tolstoy and Dostoevsky, was only to waver or flag for moments, but never to succumb. Indeed, in the 1927 essay in which he disparaged Jane Austen, Bennett listed novels which he had read "three times," the number of rereadings—albeit often mere browsings—being somehow quantitative proof of their merit; and the list included *La Cousine Bette, Le Curé de Tours, Nana,* Philippe's *Bubu de Montparnasse, Pierre et Jean,* and *The Brothers Karamazov.*

Even at the beginning, to be sure, it was not alone their realism that drew Bennett to the French. In fact, in Daudet and Balzac he sometimes found scenes that were more like romantic idylls than naturalistic photographs. Part of the lure was the strangeness of the worlds in their novels and the freedom and honesty with which they wrote of sexual passion, a topic still much veiled in English fiction before George Moore and Thomas Hardy. Nevertheless, what especially interested him at the outset was their realistic method, inconsistent though they might be, in building significance through the accumulation of objective detail; so that, if the reader patiently acquiesced for a few pages, he found himself increasingly immersed in events of no great moment individually, but of prodigious significance as part of a solid fabric. This, whether labeled realistic or naturalistic, appealed to Bennett. Unlike some others, he was not interested in finding a philosophic basis for naturalism. He always took free will for granted within a framework of circumstance, and so did not link naturalism with determinism. In short, it was not the philosophic bias of the French, but mainly their technical innovations that intrigued him. He could learn much from them while he was still trying to master the rudiments of his craft.

According to Bennett's own statement in "The Desire

for France" (in *Things That Have Interested Me*) the first French novel he read in the original was Daudet's *Fromont Jeune et Risler Ainé*. A *Journal* entry, August 6, 1907, indicates that this was about 1890. In 1903 he was to praise *Sapho* as "great and terrible," adding that "no general accusation of sentimentality can be brought against the book" (*Journal*, December 17). He also noted that he had now read "*all* the absolutely first-class French novels of the nineteenth century." Meanwhile, in 1898, he wrote that only recently had the English "absorbed from France that passion for the artistic shapely presentation of truth, and that feeling for words as words, which animated Flaubert, the Goncourts, and Maupassant, and which is so exactly described and defined in Maupassant's introduction to the collected works of Flaubert" (*Journal*, January 11). The assertion is, of course, too sweeping, as Bennett would later have admitted. Moreover, he himself was never to concentrate arduously upon his own choice of words. But what he recognized was that the art form might give interest and validity to subject matter.

In *The Truth about an Author* Bennett, in a somewhat jesting vein, told how he began to write *A Man from the North* "under the sweet influences of the de Goncourts, Turgenev, Flaubert, and de Maupassant"—as well as of George Moore (88). The novel was to consist of "*mots justes*" from Flaubert arranged in the artistic manner of the Goncourts, and it was to reveal "the Usual miraculously transformed by Art into the Sublime" (91). Since life itself was "grey, sinister and melancholy," the novel would be so, too, and its proposed title, *In the Shadow*, would be from Balzac's motto for *Le Médecin de Campagne*: "For a wounded heart, shadow and silence" (92).

According to naturalistic theory, of course, nothing was unsuited to fiction if it could be shaped into an artistic pattern. But unlike his French masters, Bennett was not willing to accept such an unqualified indifference to subject matter. In *The Book of Carlotta*, Carlotta's thoughts in the squalid bedroom of the drunken Diaz become Bennett's own means of arguing the case. Carlotta begins as a naturalist: "The eye that has learned to look life full in the face without a quiver of the lid should find nothing repulsive. Everything that is, is the ordered and calculable result of environment. Nothing can be abhorrent, nothing blameworthy, nothing contrary to nature" (223–224). So far theory prevails; but the fact remains that, despite her effort toward artistic detachment, Carlotta feels disgust: "If aught can be obscene, he was obscene" (224). Eventually, of course, Carlotta will be overcome with compassion, but pity itself is not inherent in naturalism; it is a matter on a different plane. To record the obscene required little or no art, nor could art render it profound. To unfold compassion without falling into sentimentality was the artistic challenge.

Of all authors whom Bennett admired the one whose name most often recurs in his pages is Balzac, though, to be sure, many of his remarks consist of a mere word or two of unreserved praise. Significantly, it was not primarily Balzac's realism that seems to have appealed to Bennett. In "The Fallow Fields of Fiction" (1901) he noted Balzac's "faculty for portraying communities, and for describing large co-operative activities," [14] and elsewhere he spoke of his descriptive skill. Yet, on rereading *La Cousine Bette*, in 1904, he qualified his high admiration by adding that Balzac had "not given sufficient care to the manufacture of convincing detail"; in short, he was deficient in realism (*Journal*, May 18). Two months later he noted that a story by d'Auvrevilly had "the best Balzacian romantic quality in it" (*Journal*, July 25). In 1926 he again read *La Cousine Bette* and his comment has no hint of

[14] *Ibid.*, p. 63.

interest in realism. He found the novel gripping, but "high flown and sentimental," with its "good women . . . far too good, and the bad a little too bad," and the ending was "melodramatic" (*Journal*, May 22). Finally, in 1929, in "The Progress of the Novel," he tried to give Balzac equal credit for realism and romance, and yet his phrasing favors the latter: "He beheld the human spectacle romantically, and also, in so far as his conception of realism allowed, realistically." [15]

In contrast to Balzac, whose inspiration was what Bennett really valued, the Goncourts offered primarily a precise, meticulous method of ordering observations. Their practice of keeping a journal encouraged Bennett himself to do likewise. In 1896, before *A Man from the North* had gone to press, he called himself their "latest disciple" (*Journal*, May 28). A few months later, as he read the "death of Jules" in the *Journal des Goncourts*, he remarked, ". . . the spirit of the brothers took hold of me" (*Journal*, September 29, 1896). After the funeral of Willie Boulton, his sister Tertia's fiancé, he recorded what, under the circumstances, is a rather surprising reaction: "The Goncourt brothers would in my place have noted every item of it, and particularly watched themselves. I had intended to do as much, but the various incidental distractions proved too strong for my resolution" (*Journal*, September 14, 1897). [16] In *A Man from the North, Anna of the Five Towns, The Old Wives' Tale, Clayhanger, Riceyman Steps*, and *Lord Raingo*, over a span of three decades, one finds reminiscences of the Goncourt method.

Bennett's early indebtedness to Flaubert is much less definable than that to the Goncourts, except as, like them, Flaubert kept a subdued tone while adding fact to fact. The *mot juste* was for Bennett an ideal, but he never

[15] *Ibid.*, p. 92.
[16] Cf. also letters to George Sturt in *Letters*, II, 37–38, 55–56, 66.

seriously strove to attain it. In 1914, after calling Maupassant and Flaubert both "exceptional artists," he went
on to label them "second-rate." What follows his evalua-
tion shows how little he cared for the realistic method when
it was not expressive of a compassionate mind:

> It is being discovered that Flaubert's mind was not quite
> noble enough—that, indeed, it was a cruel mind, and a
> little anaemic. *Bouvard et Pécuchet* was the crowning proof
> that Flaubert had lost sight of the humaneness of the
> world, and suffered from the delusion that he had been
> born on the wrong planet.[17]

Some pages later Bennett added that the book showed
"the lack of the sense of reality which must be the inevitable sequel of divorce from mankind" (119).

Two years later, in a burst of enthusiasm for Stendhal
and Dostoevsky, Bennett asserted that the former had
"cured me and many others of Flaubertism," even as the
latter had "cured us of Turgenevism. Both were far too
interested in life to be unduly interested in art."[18] That
last pronouncement is the clue to all Bennett's assessment
of fiction. As for Flaubert, the term "anaemic" may have
a special relevance, for it indicates what for Bennett sets
Flaubert apart from Maupassant—a distinction in which
realism is not at all the issue.

It was, indeed, Maupassant's emotional power which
had at first so enthralled Bennett as to make him overlook
defects he was to discover—and forgive—with the passing
of time. Even his sharpest criticism of Maupassant, a
Journal entry March 28, 1908, attests to his earlier worship.
The passage must be read in connection with a remark in
the preface to *The Old Wives' Tale*, the following year, in

[17] *The Author's Craft* (New York: George H. Doran, 1914), pp. 49–50.
[18] "Some Adventures among Russian Fiction," in Hynes, *The Author's Craft*, p. 119.

which Bennett wrote, "In the nineties we used to regard 'Une Vie' with mute awe."[19] Upon rereading *Une Vie*, Bennett noted in the *Journal*:

> Disappointed. No novel affected me as much as this did when I first read it about 10 or 12 years ago. It made me sad for days. Now I find it *bâclé* in parts. Too much left out—and not left out on one guiding principle but on several. The stuff not sufficiently gathered up into dramatic groupings. Recital often too ambling. Rosalie at the close rather conventional; overdrawn into a *deus ex machina*. The book too short. Sometimes too full, sometimes too hasty. But of course good.

The complaint has nothing to do with realism, and, for that matter, one may recall that Maupassant himself denied being a realist. It simply says that as a craftsman—or artist—Maupassant was not very competent. But the final verdict was still "but of course good." For in Maupassant Bennett found an attitude toward his characters that, while seemingly indifferent, ironically drew forth the reader's compassion.

In *Leonora* (1903) Bennett had already, in a way, written the life of a woman, and one may well feel here and there in the novel a resemblance to *Une Vie*. In meditating the possibility of recording yet another woman's life or possibly even the lives of two sisters, Bennett was not only indebted to Maupassant for a hint as to motif; his *Journal* sketch also suggests indebtedness for tone. For having decided to draw heavily on the actual anecdote—the antics of a crotchety "*maniaque*" in a Parisian Duval restaurant—he also thought at once of what should be his artistic attitude toward his heroine. It may well have been

[19] May 24, 1893, in a letter to Sturt, Bennett had spoken of *Bel Ami* as "one of the most obviously truthful, British-nation-shocking, disgusting, attractive, overwhelmingly-powerful novels I ever read" (*Letters*, II, 7).

of Maupassant that he was thinking when he noted that the first scene should be "written rather cruelly" (*Journal,* November 18, 1903). He did not, of course, carry out his initial intent in the story of the Baines sisters, nor did he approach the severity of Maupassant; but certainly at times in both *The Old Wives' Tale* and *Clayhanger* an outward casualness reminiscent of Maupassant accentuates one's sense of the smoldering passions of the characters. Perhaps Bennett's most accurate statement of what Maupassant represented for him is in a pocket philosophy, *Mental Efficiency,* where in a passing remark, and using the adjective in its proper meaning, he speaks of "that terrible novel 'Fort comme la Mort.'" [20]

In *Things That Have Interested Me,* Bennett found Maupassant narrower than Chekhov in "his interests and his sympathies," but he concluded: "still in the emotional power of rendering a given situation de Maupassant is perhaps the superior to the other; assuredly he is not his inferior. And does anything else finally count?" (207). In the same essay, "Short Stories," he found in certain works of Maupassant a "perfection of masterful technique," but what he especially valued was his "sheer creative force" (207, 208).

Théophile Gautier's name does not appear in the published *Journal,* and the reference to him in *The Book of Carlotta* is interesting mainly for what it tells about Bennett himself. He manages gratuitously to drag in an allusion by having Carlotta remark that from Gautier she learned "the new truth that in the body, and the instincts of the body, there should be no shame, but rather a frank, joyous pride" (15). Unquestionably, Bennett liked the new truth, which he found, too, of course, in Balzac, Maupassant, and perhaps most of all in Zola. Yet he really

[20] *Mental Efficiency and Other Hints to Men and Women* (New York: George H. Doran, 1911), p. 61.

could not use it literally. He could let Carlotta do things that no respectable Victorian woman would have done, but she is drawn to Diaz not at all through a joyous pride in sensuality, but purportedly through spiritual inspiration.

Next to Balzac and Maupassant, the nineteenth-century French author whom Bennett appears to have read most was Zola. To be sure, if we remember that he often skimmed books or dipped into them here and there to examine their technique, even the inclusion of *Nana* among those which he had read three times may not mean a great immersion in Zola. He could not learn much from him that he could not get better from the Goncourts, and he himself did not care in his own writing—even in *Riceyman Steps* or *The Pretty Lady*—to depict at length the ugly and sordid. He read *L'Assommoir* early, [21] presumably interested mainly in its subject matter. In 1904 he noted that, though "very earnest and meticulous," it was unrealistic in one scene and "distressingly forced and clumsy, with its artificial 'preparation'" in another (*Journal*, October 5). In contrast, a year later he was enthusiastic about *L'Oeuvre* despite its carelessness. He called it a "colossal affair . . . so serious, tremendous, and imposing." The last part, involving a subject of special interest to a writer, the "fight between love and art," was "simply magnificent": in it Zola had "stepped into the heroic" (*Journal*, November 7, 1905). Here once again Bennett was essentially talking not about naturalism, but about a novelist's creative vision.

His eventual opinion of the typical naturalistic novel comes out in a summation in *The Author's Craft* (1914): "The notion that 'naturalists' have at last lighted on a final formula which ensures truth to life is ridiculous" (58). To be sure, in 1928 the best thing he could say about

[21] *The Truth about an Author*, p. 30.

Mansfield Park—other than that it was a "fine novel"—was that it had "one or two pages of Zola's or rather Huysmans's realism in it" (*Journal*, July 18). However, shortly afterward, in "The Progress of the Novel," he refused to credit Zola with originality: "Zola carried the novel no farther than Balzac. He did nothing new. He was not a pioneer, an explorer, a discoverer. He was merely a supercraftsman of unsurpassed energy and tenacity of purpose who knew how to organise his terrific energy, and who had hours of genius." [22]

Like Gautier, Huysmans was more a symbol to Bennett than a novelist to be studied seriously. His instinctive feeling toward him appears to have been one of revulsion. In "The Fallow Fields of Fiction" (1901), he calls *La Cathédrale* a "finicking and egotistic novel . . . in which the unsurpassed beauty of Chartres is degraded to the uses of an arena for the antics of a diseased soul." [23] In contrast, in *Whom God Hath Joined* (1906), Mark Ridware casually mentions the fact that his brother Lawrence—whose wife is utterly vicious—is an authority on Huysmans's novels. Finally, in *The Author's Craft*, apparently with no change of opinion on *La Cathédrale*, Bennett defended *En Menage* and the descriptive essays *De Tout:* "Both reproduce with exasperation what is generally regarded as the sordid ugliness of commonplace daily life. Yet both exercise a unique charm (and will surely be read when *La Cathédrale* is forgotten)" (44). Apparently in these, *Au Rebours*, and *La Bas*, Bennett found nothing diseased, and he was undisturbed by their melodramatic sordidness. Perhaps as much as anything else, the subject matter of Huysmans represented liberation from British Victorianism.

Had Bennett really been willing to value art for its own sake, he would have progressed from admiration of the

[22] Hynes, *The Author's Craft*, pp. 92–93.
[23] *Ibid.*, p. 57.

Goncourts to fascination with Proust. Not that Proust is to be fitted into the naturalistic tradition, but that Bennett did have to admit the validity of his analytic method. In 1926, for example, he wrote: "About two-thirds of Proust's work must be devoted to the minutiae of social manners, the rendering ridiculous of a million varieties of snob. At this game Proust is a master." [24] He could not make up his mind, however, whether to offer praise or to admit that he really cared very little for Proust. Thus in this same essay he considered *A l'ombre des jeunes filles en fleurs* a "fearful fall" from "*Swann.*" In his *Journal* for August 23, 1926, somewhere near the time when he wrote this, having called *A l'ombre* "a bit on the dry side, though very good," he continued: "It doesn't impassion *me*. I couldn't care much if I didn't read any more of it. It lacks juice. It has almost no concern with anything except analysis of views and feelings—especially snobbishness. No landscapes, no furniture, no corporate life. No general 'feel' of things."

A few years earlier Bennett had pronounced Proust "unreadable" and accused him of writing "the same book over and over again, at greater length and with ever-increasing refinement and finickingness." [25] And in "Some French Books," included in *The Savour of Life* (1928), he wrote, "Proust has enchanted me, and he has bored me" (160). In 1929 he called him both "great" and "tedious," and denied him originality, even in the realm of psychology, in spite of his "passion for the minutiae" of it. And he climaxed his charge with "as for his scope, it is unquestionably narrow; no novelist has built higher walls than his." [26] What these ambivalent and sometimes anguished comments on Proust add up to is: method—of

[24] "Marcel Proust," in *Things That Have Interested Me: Third Series*, p. 165.
[25] *Things That Have Interested Me* (*Second Series*), pp. 35, 41.
[26] "The Progress of the Novel," in Hynes, *The Author's Craft*, p. 96.

course, incontestably significant; substance—not, after all, really vital. They are, now, the inquiring suggestions of an artist concerned with improvement as a craftsman; but, again, the exasperated, hence oversevere pronouncement of the plain man who, when confronted with subject matter remote from his own personal interest, says, "Let the art go hang!"

During his discipleship to the French realists Bennett was also immersing himself in the novels of George Moore, who, for Bennett, could do little that was wrong. In Moore he discovered about as great a freedom in depicting the relations of the sexes as in Moore's French masters, and also a methodical building up of evidence as in the Goncourts. In addition, he was much more attuned to Moore's subject matter. Eventually, too, he was to cite his works when discussing the importance of beauty in literature.

In his *Journal*, January 12, 1897, he noted that he was reading *Mike Fletcher*, and in the book itself he wrote, "vicious, meretricious and—delicious." The next year he read *Evelyn Innes*, and Moore's name recurs frequently in the *Journal* down through the years. In an essay "Mr. George Moore," Bennett momentarily forgot *Clarissa* and called *A Modern Lover* "the first realistic novel in England."[27] Here as elsewhere he stressed Moore's concern for beauty. In 1904, in the free-swinging essay "My Literary Heresies," he asked whether *A Mummer's Wife*, *A Drama in Muslin*, and *Sister Teresa* were not "three of the greatest novels of their century."[28] The second he later called a "masterpiece" on the middle class.[29] Like *Une*

---

[27] *Fame and Fiction: An Enquiry into Certain Popularities* (London: Grant Richards, 1901), p. 249. The volume is composed of articles in the *Academy*, 1899–1900.

[28] Hynes, *The Author's Craft*, p. 240.

[29] *Books and Persons: Being Comments on a Past Epoch 1908–1911* (New York: George H. Doran, 1917), February 4, 1909. The articles composing the volume appeared in the *New Age*, 1908–1911.

Vie, the first, *A Mummer's Wife*, stretches over years of a woman's life. But more reminiscent of *L'Assommoir* than of Maupassant, it takes the heroine almost steadily downward, with no significant reversal and with variation only as to the squalor, sordidness, and repulsiveness of her decline. It is difficult to see why Bennett should have heralded it as a skillful work of art. To be sure, in any given scene it is vivid, and, of course, if one yields himself to it, it is pathetic. Its weakness is that the succession of shocks with little variation soon becomes monotonous. Possibly because of the rapidity with which Bennett hurried through novels he was not disturbed by the repetition. In any event, he was eager to have a British champion of a new way of writing and a new subject matter, and Moore represented both.

In the *Journal* there is only one reference to George Gissing, a secondhand account from Wells of the distressing circumstances of his death (July 31, 1904). Nor is Gissing mentioned in most of Bennett's critical excursions among novels. Yet one of his earliest and best statements of his own literary ideal is a discussion of Gissing. The passage may be overgenerous to Gissing, and it may not really distinguish between the virtues of realism and those of romanticism; but it does tell what a good realistic novel should do:

> To take the common grey things which people know and despise, and, without tampering, to disclose their epic significance, their essential grandeur—that is realism, as distinguished from idealism or romanticism. It may scarcely be, it probably is not, the greatest of all; but it is art, precious and indisputable. Such art has Mr. Gissing accomplished. In *The Nether World*, his most characteristic book, the myriad squalid futilities of an industrial quarter of London are gathered up into a large coherent movement of which the sinister and pathetic

beauty is but too stringently apparent. After *The Nether World* Clerkenwell is no longer negligible. It has import. You feel the sullen and terrible pulse of this universe which lies beneath your own. You may even envy the blessedness of the meek, and perceive in the lassitude of the heavy laden a secret grace that can never be yours.[30]

Bennett would certainly have been pleased some years later if his own story of Rachel in *The Price of Love* had been similarly reviewed, and in his servant girl Elsie he sought to reveal a "secret grace" in the "blessedness of the meek."

When Bennett exalted *Clarissa* as a realistic novel he was, of course, thinking of its psychological revelations. He could also find a limited psychological analysis in such a romance writer as Stevenson,[31] and in 1904 he became enthusiastic over the depiction of a young girl's thoughts and feelings in the rather romantic *Les Liaisons Dangereuses*, the eighteenth-century story in letter form by Chodorlos de Laclos (*Journal*, March 10). It was the Russians, however, who offered him both a vast realistic social canvas and, especially Dostoevsky, a psychological examination of individual characters. What they also provided is revealed in a passage in *The Savour of Life* (1928). Reasserting his view that "the twelve finest novels are all Russian," he credited them with "the best sort of realism—namely, the realism which is combined with a comprehending charity of judgment. Also, in the main, their creations are more heroical in scale" (128).

Bennett implied that he first read Dostoevsky in the early 1890's, and he knew Turgenev from at least as early. Though he was later to write that Dostoevsky cured Bennett's generation of Turgenevism, he meant only that Turgenev had been revered too much for his rigorous

[30] "Mr. Gissing," in *Fame and Fiction*, pp. 201–202.
[31] *Journal*, May 21, 1896, and January 19, 1904.

artistic method, and that in paying more heed to what he had to say than to the novelistic art Dostevsky had made fiction a more passionate and inclusive expression of life. Nevertheless, as we shall note later, he always felt the compassion and the melancholy in Turgenev, as he did usually, though to a lesser degree in Chekhov.

Turgenev, on whom he wrote an essay in 1899, included in *Fame and Fiction*, had an intangible influence upon his craftsmanship while he was still deeply immersed in the French realists. In a letter to George Sturt, February 18, 1896, Bennett wrote, "Man, we have more to learn in mere technique from Turgenev than from any other soul."[32] March 8, 1896, he again wrote Sturt that Turgenev, "having conceived his story, deliberatcly strips it of every picturesque inessential, austerely turns aside from any artfulness, and seeks to present it in the simplest most straightforward form."[33]

When Wells told Bennett that *Anna of the Five Towns* was an "under-developed" photograph, he replied: "But I trust you understand that the degree of development to which I have brought the photograph, is what I think the proper degree. It is Turgenev's degree, and Flaubert's. It is *not* Balzac's."[34] In short, it was Turgenev's restraint and the subtlety of his nuances that Bennett admired, and *Anna* was certainly the better for his influence.

Of Chekhov Bennett was sometimes critical, but in a review of *The Cherry Orchard* in 1911 he spoke of the play's daring naturalism and called it "one of the most savage and convincing satires on a whole society that was ever seen in the theatre."[35] To the poetic beauty in Chekhov we shall return later.

[32] *Letters*, II, 36.
[33] *Ibid.*, p. 38.
[34] *Arnold Bennett and H. G. Wells*, September 20, 1902, p. 89.
[35] "Chekhov's *Cherry Orchard*," in Hynes, *The Author's Craft*, p. 247.

On Tolstoy Bennett was ambivalent. In his *Journal*, April 24, 1913, he mentioned having completed *War and Peace* two days earlier, and after praising especially the battle of Borodino, the Rostov family, and "'set' descriptions of Russian life," he climaxed his note: "Terrific book. I wanted to write one of the same dimensions. And the final thrills of it *did* inspire me to a good basic scheme for the foundations of the third *Clayhanger*." In contrast, after a while he wearied of *Anna Karenina*, finding it badly constructed, dull, and too much dependent on "externals." But in the same article in which he condemned it in 1916 he again lauded *War and Peace*, especially its "unsentimentalized annals of the home life of Pierre and Natasha after all the battles are over." [36] It was in such scenes, of course, that Tolstoy was nearest to Balzac, and also, though culturally far removed, nearest in substance to Bennett's own fiction. [37]

It is not possible to identify any specific influence of Dostoevsky upon Bennett, mainly because Bennett himself did not burrow into the minds of his characters or let himself go emotionally. But especially from 1910 onward Dostoevsky's name appears repeatedly when Bennett speaks of genius. Essentially he represented for him the ideal novelist—the man who is, first of all, absorbed in probing the nature of the human predicament and who finds art the truest means for exploring it. Having dealt with Dostoevsky as one of the greatest of the psychological realists, Bennett, without the least inconsistency, wrote in his 1916 article that *The Brothers Karamazov* was "both more true and more romantic than any other [novel] whatsoever." [38]

Indeed, though he found the words "realistic" and

[36] "Some Adventures among Russian Fiction," in *ibid.*, p. 117.
[37] A *Journal* entry April 4, 1927, calls Gorky's *Decadence* "very fine."
[38] Hynes, *The Author's Craft*, p. 118.

"romantic" useful, as we all do, in 1921 Bennett wrote to Hugh Walpole, "I don't know what you mean by 'romantic.' All the big realists are romantic." Citing Balzac, Chekhov, and Dostoevsky, he affirmed: "There is no opposition or mutual-excluding between romance & realism. Believe me."[39]

Honesty was the first requirement for a work of art, and whether romantic or realistic, a novel must first be judged for its integrity. The foremost and unpardonable sin against honesty was sentimentality. This for Bennett was the bête noire. It was indeed a sin which he himself seldom committed in his serious writing, though he could not have pleaded innocent in regard to some of his lighter work. After he retreated from his initial devotion to the French realists he began to discover even among them a penchant for the sentimental, sometimes disguised by a mask of severity and objectivity, sometimes unashamed.

So it was that, though pronouncing *Germinal* a "fine" novel, he yet found its climax "marred by a false sentimentality, which is none the less sentimentality for being sensual."[40] Even Balzac could not be exonerated, despite the persistence with which Bennett maintained his genius. May 8, 1926, he devoted a long paragraph in his *Journal* to Balzac's deficiencies. After 140 pages of *Le Lys dans la Vallée*, he was giving the book up. Among its other defects were its "sentimentalism and *sensiblerie* and eloquence"; and its heroine was far too angelic. Yet Bennett remembered that thirty years earlier he had "enjoyed it immensely and thought it was a masterpiece." He had also lost his admiration for *Le Curé de Tours* and *Père Goriot*, now finding them thin and tedious; and he remarked that, if *Splendeurs et Misères* or *La Cousine Bette* would not restore his respect, he would "denounce Balzac as a back number, to my

[39] Letter dated November 22, 1921 (*Letters*, III, 150).
[40] "The Midlands," in *Paris Nights*, p. 285.

extreme regret." Of course, Balzac could withstand even this onslaught and still be for Bennett a genius.

Naturally enough Bennett found sentimentality in almost all the popular British novelists of his own time, who played to the predilections of their readers. In *A Man from the North* Adeline is a well-meaning young woman, but her reading of the sentimental *East Lynne* leads Richard to the reflection "How commonplace must she be!" (89). It was the Adelines, of course, who supported the popular novelists. In *Fame and Fiction* (1901) Bennett depreciated Barrie for being a sentimentalist, and he bluntly attributed Kipling's popularity to his "constant abuse and falsification of sentiment" (15). His stock examples of insincerity and sentimentality, whose names recur over the years, were Mrs. Humphry Ward, Hall Caine, Marie Corelli, and especially Charlotte Yonge. In *Clayhanger* Edwin's sister Maggie, like Adeline a well-intentioned person, exhibits her cultural starvation by reading Charlotte Yonge.

But more significantly, in his revolt against Victorianism Bennett perceived sentimentality of varying kinds among the famous nineteenth-century British novelists. In *Books and Persons* he wrote: "The damning fault of all mid-Victorian novels is that they are incurably ugly and sentimental. Novelists had not yet discovered that the first business of a work of art is to be beautiful, and its second not to be sentimental" (September, 1910). In 1927 he remained of the same opinion: "English novels in general, even the masterpieces, are rendered insular for me by our racial sentimentality and prudery."[41] In 1909 he had remarked that, being a woman, George Eliot "dared not write an entirely honest novel!" He had continued: "Nor a man either! Between Fielding and Meredith no entirely

[41] "On Re-reading the English Novelists," in Hynes, *The Author's Craft*, p. 254.

honest novel was written by anybody in England. The
fear of the public, the lust of popularity, feminine prudery,
sentimentalism, Victorian niceness—one or other of these
things prevented honesty." [42] His standard was Fielding,
the French and Russians, and, besides Meredith, such
authors as Hardy, Samuel Butler, and Wells.

There was no special reason why Bennett should have
cared for Sir Walter Scott, and, though he included him
in his 1904 list of great authors, he did not. His strongest
animadversion is later, in his article in 1927 "On Re-
reading the English Novelists." With characteristic
positiveness he writes, "Scott I will not read." He credits
him with some historical importance and approves of the
first two-thirds of *The Heart of Midlothian*, but he finds him
possessed of "the country-gentleman mind . . . unsuited to
a creative artist." [43] Among the connotations of the epithet
in its context is a sentimental evasion of harsh realities.
Bennett's feelings about Thackeray were very similar. In
1904, in "My Literary Heresies," he had written that
Thackeray "could never look life steadily in the face,
because he was a bit of a snob and wholly a sentimentalist." [44] In "On Re-reading" he renewed his attack of more
than twenty years earlier. Even *Vanity Fair*, which he
admitted to be a "great novel," was disfigured by "com-
promise between falsity and truth." [45]

Of all Bennett's major English predecessors it was
Dickens whom he could least endure. In *The Truth about an
Author* he noted that he was thirty years old when he first
read *David Copperfield*. In "My Literary Heresies" he
considered Dickens "devoid of a feeling for beauty and a
feeling for literature," and he went so far as to accuse him

---

[42] *Books and Persons*, May 27, 1909.
[43] Hynes, *The Author's Craft*, p. 255.
[44] *Ibid.*, p. 236.
[45] *Ibid.*, p. 258.

of making a "constant search for ugliness." Dickens had "no natural distinction of mind," and his pathos was "merely comic, and an absolute proof that his conception of pathos was the conception of a milliner's apprentice." [46] In fact, he actually listed by number seven types of deficiency in Dickens and asserted that his works would probably not survive. In 1910 he found *Dombey and Son* "appallingly vulgar—there is no other word." [47] In *The Author's Craft* (1914) he linked Dickens with Thackeray as having a "common" texture of mind and maintained that he "fell short in courageous facing of the truth, and in certain delicacies of perception" (47). In his rapid review in "On Re-reading" he admitted that Dickens was a "great creative genius," but protested that he had "never been able to read a novel of Dickens from beginning to end." [48] In *The Savour of Life*, published the next year, he repeated his charge, almost a boast, saying that he had tried unsuccessfully with at least twenty novels. According to Mrs. Bennett, it was Dickens's "insincerity" to which Bennett vehemently objected: "'You see,' he once said to me, 'you can *feel* that Dickens is underneath everything, a voluptuary. And he covers it up the whole time with his dreadful untrue stuff.'" [49]

Yet, with much justification Sacheverell Sitwell remarks that Bennett's "literary achievement descended in direct line from Dickens, from the later Dickens." [50] And J. B. Atkins has quipped, "When he told me, to my sorrow, that he could not read Dickens, I fancied that if Dickens had written in French Arnold would have read him rapturously." [51] When one recalls the numerous charming

[46] *Ibid.*, p. 235.
[47] *Florentine Journal*, May 16, 1910.
[48] Hynes, *The Author's Craft*, p. 257.
[49] D. C. Bennett, *Arnold Bennett*, p. 103.
[50] *Florentine Journal*, p. 10.
[51] Atkins, *Incidents and Reflections*, p. 175.

fluff-headed girls in Bennett's light stories, old Mr. Shushions in *Clayhanger*, or aspects of Elsie that resemble nothing in the Goncourts' or Balzac's servant girls, one is inclined to think first of all of Dickens. Can it be that, even as Conrad most deplored Dostoevsky, whom he at times tended to parallel, Bennett exaggerated in Dickens a tendency toward which he was inclined? Still the charge of sentimentality remains; not that Bennett himself was never sentimental, but he kept a close guard against insincerity, even in such theatrical works as *The Book of Carlotta* and *The Pretty Lady*.

The subtitle of *The Savour of Life* (1928) is "Essays in Gusto." The term "gusto" well characterizes Bennett's lifelong approach to literature. He could plunge through badly written pages with zest if he sensed vitality in a novel. Though he once used the label "professional squad" to include Bradley, Herford, Dowden, Elton, and Walter Raleigh, as well as Saintsbury, his indignation was directed especially at Saintsbury,[52] and his complaint was that Saintsbury had no interest in what literature was for.[53] In contrast, he was enthusiastic about Hazlitt's "famous essay on the nature of 'poetry in general.'"[54] Hazlitt, of course, had uninhibited gusto.

If a work of fiction were to have vitality, it must be drawn from life as the novelist knew it. Hence, in *The Author's Craft* (1914) Bennett asserted, "First-class fiction is, and must be, in the final resort autobiographical" (60). Fielding was an example, and, allowing for the transformation in art, so were Balzac and the Russians. The fact that Bennett himself wrote his observations in a journal

[52] *Books and Persons*, October 27, 1910.

[53] *Literary Taste*, p. 13. Later he withdrew his condemnation when, upon reading "a lot" of the *History of the French Novel*, he found that Saintsbury illuminated fictional technique and that his learning was "staggering" (*Journal*, December 26, 1917).

[54] *How to Live on Twenty-Four Hours a Day*, p. 92.

and that he admired Pepys [55] is sufficient evidence that he recognized even in the raw matter of life—selected, to be sure, but not substantially altered—the interest and values he looked for first of all in fiction. And, of course, the Five-Towns novels drew in part on what he knew from personal experience.

When Bennett praised Balzac he focused on the dynamic quality of his work. When he demurred, as in casual aspersion of *Seraphita*, it was often because he chanced to find him dull. [56] He had early approved of his and Scott's melodrama, [57] and in his *Journal*, April 7, 1913, he revealed that he could endure much in Balzac for the sake of what really mattered: "Balzac was an ignorant and a crude man, often childish in his philosophizing. But if he had been properly educated and influenced he would have been a great social philosopher. His *aperçus* are often astounding. And his vitality is terrific."

In "The Paper Cap" Bennett has his hero settle himself comfortably on his yacht and pick up a volume of Balzac, "the most human and the most grandiose of all novelists." [58] The adjective was never a pejorative for Bennett. He could even admire Disraeli as a "grandiose adventurer, not merely in politics, but with a pen." [59] And, having found *Coningsby* a "sad welter," he went on to commend it as "very rich and varied." [60] Such comments do not smack of Marcus Aurelius; they do represent that aspect of Bennett's nature that created the fantasias for their sheer exuberant fun.

[55] *Self and Self-Management: Essays about Existing* (New York: George H. Doran, 1918), p. 45.

[56] "Virginia Woolf's *Orlando*" (1928), in Hynes, *The Author's Craft*, p. 223.

[57] *Fame and Fiction*, p. 114.

[58] *Elsie and the Child*, p. 104.

[59] "On Re-reading," in Hynes, *The Author's Craft*, p. 261.

[60] *Journal*, August 25, 1927. In *The Savour of Life* Bennett again called Disraeli grandiose, and he added, "Also he could do the purple passage" (167).

In the numerous references which Bennett made to Dostoevsky there is no discussion of the philosophic intricacies that have fascinated other students of his work. It does not appear that Bennett tried to establish the symbolic nature of any of the characters in *The Brothers Karamazov* or to pursue the implications of their speeches. He, of course, regarded the novel as a much subtler psychological study than *War and Peace*, in which the descriptions of externals sufficed for him. But what caused him to return to the work was the emotional intensity of the internal conflicts of the characters. This he could sense even if not immersed in the philosophic questions and psychological complexities which their conduct might suggest. In short, it was its vitality that finally led Bennett to call *The Brothers Karamazov* "the greatest novel ever written." [61]

Bennett's approval could be far-ranging. In 1904 he even pronounced *Fanny Hill* a "masterpiece of pornographic literature" (*Journal*, December 14); and of Swinburne's *Poems and Ballads* he wrote that it was "fine in sensuality." [62] Mere sensuality had no interest for Bennett, and, of course, there was much more to Swinburne as later to D. H. Lawrence, whom Bennett pronounced "first-rate" at his best. [63] Again, however, he sensed the liveliness in the unfolding of human passions. More truly representative of what he wanted—an honest depiction of the whole nature of man—was the poetry of Walt Whitman. In 1904 he discovered "much in common" between Emerson and Whitman (*Journal*, January 4). Once when accusing Anatole France of "spiritual anaemia," he suggested that one should "wake him by throwing 'Leaves of Grass' or

[61] "André Gide's *Dostoevsky*," in *Things That Have Interested Me: Third Series*, p. 108.

[62] *Books and Persons*, April 22, 1909.

[63] *The Savour of Life*, p. 302.

'Ecce Homo' at his head."[64] And in *These Twain* Clay-hanger, a plain man in his reading habits, likes Whitman. In his *Journal*, January 27, 1905, Bennett spoke of Twain's *Life on the Mississippi* as new to him, and he labeled it "fine, amusing, interesting." In *Your United States* it be-came an "incomparable masterpiece" (108); and in 1921 it was Twain's "greatest masterpiece."[65] It was, in fact, a book which Bennett could read with gusto.

Among his contemporaries Wells was a perennial favorite in spite of his disregard for the rules of artistic craftsmanship. A comment in 1909 is typical: "Human nature—you get it pretty complete in 'Tono-Bungay,' the entire tableau."[66] In *The Savour of Life* he was enthusiastic about Maugham's *Of Human Bondage*. Having praised Cohan's *Little Millionaire* for its honesty "beneath the blatancy,"[67] he later rated Cohan far above O'Neill, whom he considered sentimental.[68] In all these writers there was something of the same appeal that Bennett found in the music halls. Much could be overlooked if there was vigor.

Having asserted that truth to life was essential and that the principal characters must be convincing, Bennett chose Sinclair Lewis's *Babbitt* over *Main Street*. The heroine in the latter was a "sentimental stick"; Babbitt, in contrast, was a "genuine individual that all can recognize for reality."[69] In *Elmer Gantry* he was struck with the "very vivacious idiomatic slang."[70] And in "The Progress of the Novel" he

[64] *Books and Persons*, October 29, 1908. In the same article, though admit-ting that *Ecce Homo* was "conceited," Bennett still called it a "great book, full of great things." Presumably he was impressed by its stimulation without pursuing its logic.
[65] *Things That Have Interested Me*, p. 148.
[66] *Books and Persons*, March 4, 1909.
[67] *Your United States*, p. 141.
[68] *Things That Have Interested Me: Third Series*, p. 26.
[69] *Ibid.*, p. 161.
[70] *The Savour of Life*, p. 124.

linked Lewis and Dreiser as a "pair of mighty destroyers,"
though he added that they seemed to have little energy left
for "implicit reconstruction." [71] Certainly he was again
very much the plain man in endorsing *Babbitt* and *Elmer
Gantry*.

It was Theodore Dreiser, however, who best among
late-comers gave Bennett the vitality that he wanted. In
his *Journal*, December 7, 1916, he spoke of being satisfied
with what he had written of his new novel, *The Roll Call*,
and he continued, "Undoubtedly I have been refreshed
and invigorated by reading Dreiser's *The Financier*, which
absolutely held me." In that entry he labeled *The Titan*
"not so good," but three days earlier he had praised it
"despite its dreadful slovenliness in details of phrase." [72]
More than nine years later, after 150 pages of *An American
Tragedy*, Bennett admitted that "the mere writing is simply
bloody-careless, clumsy, terrible." However, he continued: "But there is power, and he holds you, because his
big construction is good. The book quite woke me up last
night just as I was going off to sleep" (*Journal*, May 23,
1926). An entry a few days later speaks of the "fineness"
and "originality" of its psychology (May 29). Four days
later Bennett repeated his praise of the psychology and
concluded, "This must be one of the very finest American
novels" (June 2). Finally, in *The Savour of Life*, though he
found *Sister Carrie* "marred by sentimentality," he remarked
that twenty-six years earlier he had reviewed it "with
enthusiasm" (305). He again praised *The Financier* and
unreservedly credited *An American Tragedy* with "an
absolutely fearless adherence to truth and a terrific
imaginative power" (304). Indeed, Bennett took pride in
having urged the British public to acclaim Dreiser. He
found in his pages a new and vast world, even as, years

[71] Hynes, *The Author's Craft*, p. 95.
[72] Letter to Mrs. Elsie Herzog, December 4, 1916 (*Letters*, III, 22).

before, he had found one in Balzac, Maupassant, Zola, and George Moore. It was a crude world, crudely delineated, but it was able to wake men up.

If it is admitted that all the novels which Bennett called "great," "magnificent," or "terrific" were lively and interesting, the fact must not go unnoticed that he was also unable to appreciate certain novels which were also intensely alive, but in a quiet or obscure way. We have already noticed his ambivalence concerning Proust, which came essentially from his unwillingness to work out the intricacies in his patterns and to be alert to the nuances and echoes which gave artistic grace to his pages. Bennett's weakness lay in his insistence on "readability," which meant that a novel at its first, and often highly rapid, reading should yield much of its substance. One should not need to pore over it. In the cardlike article "My Literary Heresies" (1904), Bennett put the issue frankly and naïvely. Protesting that in *The Ring and the Book* Browning had forced his reader overmuch to struggle with his meaning, he continued:

> It is useless to say: "Ah! But you shirk the intellectual labour!" Yes, I do, because the end of art is to please the aesthetic sense, and it is impossible that the aesthetic sense should remain in a condition to be pleased while the intellectual faculty is at full stretch.[73]

The argument here is about as useful as Mark Twain's that what he liked was as good as what anybody else liked, for Bennett was reducing aesthetic pleasure to mere instant response. Of course, he was fortunately unwilling to push the logic to its ultimate absurdity, and so he never actually condemned subtle writing; he merely refused to spend much time on it, even when grudgingly admitting its merits.

[73] Hynes, *The Author's Craft*, p. 234.

Sometimes when he really liked a work he was still astray. Thus he pronounced "Rappacini's Daughter" to be "in the Poe manner," hardly a discriminating perception (*Journal*, July 24, 1907). Again, his comments on the structure and technique of a novel may only cover the surface. When, for example, he concluded that Conrad's *The Secret Agent* gave a "disappointing effect of slightness" (*Journal*, September 25, 1907), one wonders how well he grasped what Conrad was trying to tell. And as late as 1927, in his article "On Re-reading the English Novelists," all he could say about *Tristram Shandy* was that it was "too individual and too capricious."[74]

Meredith is a quite good measure of Bennett's appreciation. In "My Literary Heresies" he questioned whether *Harry Richmond* or *The Egoist* was Meredith's best work, and in 1928, in an article "The Meredith Centenary," he admitted *Beauchamp's Career* to their company. But he complained of being unable, even with effort, to finish other Meredithian novels. In his usual dogmatic way he pronounced the reason: "Meredith has not mastered thought."[75] From the beginning, on the other hand, he had praised *Evan Harrington*, a fine novel, to be sure, but perhaps the easiest of all Meredith's works to understand. Writing of Olive Schreiner's *The Story of an African Farm*, he named it and *Evan Harrington* as two of the "three novels that have kept me up all night."[76]

What was Bennett to do with Henry James? He could not reject him outright; in fact, he had to admit that he was superior. But having done that, he joined the large number, including William James and H. G. Wells, who accounted as faults the very qualities which James himself most cherished. An early pronouncement is

[74] *Ibid.*, p. 255.
[75] *Ibid.*, p. 126.
[76] *The Savour of Life*, p. 309.

encouraging, but ambiguous. In a paragraph review of *Embarrassments*, in 1896, Bennett called "The Figure in the Carpet" "exceedingly subtle and exceedingly clear," and he placed himself among James's admirers.[77] One may, to be sure, demur on the clarity of the story, and since the review does not define the figure, it is not certain that Bennett penetrated the subtlety. In 1905, on Wells's recommendation, he waded through 150 pages of *The Ambassadors* and noted in his *Journal* that the writing was "merely perfect." He gave up, however, with the verdict "But I found the plot clumsily managed and a very considerable absence of passionate feeling" (January 11). Here again was the plain man's natural response. What Bennett could not perceive was that, as with Browning, the flame of passion might spring up from a rarefied intellectual kindling.

A review of *The Finer Grain* in 1910 is mainly negative. Bennett found James "tremendously lacking in emotional power" and in his view of life "at bottom conventional, timid, and undecided."[78] In 1927, in "A Candid Opinion of Henry James," he virtually boasted that he had "honestly enjoyed" only *In the Cage* and *The Other House*. As if to reject the cogency of contrary arguments, he was willing to grant that James "knew everything about writing novels—except how to keep my attention."[79] Reiterating similar points in *The Savour of Life*, he put candidly the real issue that separated him and James: "I think that in the fastidiousness of his taste he rather repudiated life" (120).[80] That word "fastidiousness" is the key. It is, of course, unjust, but it marks the difference in the temperaments of the two novelists. The rest of the sentence is also unjust.

[77] "Henry James's *Embarrassments*," in Hynes, *The Author's Craft*, p. 129.
[78] "Henry James's *The Finer Grain*," in *ibid.*, p. 131.
[79] *Ibid.*, p. 133.
[80] Cf. also *Things That Have Interested Me*, pp. 324 and 329–330, where Bennett says that James's novels "lack ecstasy, guts."

We have simply to recognize that Bennett did not want to take the time really to understand James.

"Beauty" is a convenient nebulous term, and Bennett fell back upon it from time to time. He insisted that a novel must be beautiful even while depicting realistic or naturalistic truth. A way of solving the matter was to resort to rhetoric, as when he recorded in his *Journal*, "All ugliness has an aspect of beauty" (January 3, 1899), or agreed with Rodin that "everything on earth is beautiful" (May 6, 1906). The novelist's function, he once wrote, was to find coherence amidst "incoherence, to give shape to the amorphous, to discover beauty which was hidden, to reveal essential truth."[81] Despite the fact that such statements are truisms, Bennett's instinct for beauty in fiction was not without direction.

Mere plot and realistic authenticity would not suffice in a novel. Bennett insisted upon lyric overtones, without which a story was flat and lacking in charm. It was such a lack that he regretted in Zola and in such diverse novelists and dramatists as Kipling, Ibsen, Anatole France, Galsworthy, and Shaw. Of Kipling he remarked, in "My Literary Heresies," that his "feeling for beauty" was "but faint."[82] Preeminent among his strictures on Ibsen's *The Wild Duck* was that "it never strikes one as beautiful" (*Journal*, May 5, 1906). He was still willing to consider Ibsen important in the growth of realism. In Anatole France's *L'Histoire Comique* the sensuality was objectionable,[83] which is to say that it was ugly.

Bennett was exceptionally harsh with Galsworthy, though in 1914 he wrote Mrs. Herzog that he liked *The Dark Flower*. In "Galsworthy's *A Commentary*" (1908), he denied that either that work or *The Man of Property*

---

[81] *Fame and Fiction*, pp. 38–39.
[82] Hynes, *The Author's Craft*, p. 240.
[83] *Books and Persons*, October 29, 1908.

possessed a "sense of beauty." [84] The next year, in "A Few Words on Galsworthy," he wrote with oversimplification, "Novelists present superficial ugliness in such a way as to give the pleasure of beauty; so do painters." [85] He then went on to find Galsworthy, Granville Barker, and even the scene painter remiss aesthetically in the second act of *Strife*. The same year he called Shaw honest, but "deficient in a feeling for beauty and in emotion." [86] It is significant that Thomas Hardy protested that both Zola and Ibsen were deficient in beauty, and later students have concurred on the flatness of too much of Kipling and Galsworthy.

As for examples of authors in whose works Bennett found beauty, we can begin with Shakespeare. Reading good poetry, like listening to music, inspired him for his own composition. Hence, he noted in his *Journal* for December 8, 1903, that he had read the first act of *Othello*—presumably reread it—and he remarked quite simply, ". . . and it did me good" and, although he did not read extensively in poetry, he also liked Thomson's *The Seasons* and, as we have noticed, Wordsworth and even Crashaw. But he was much more interested in poetic fiction, for he saw life essentially in a narrative pattern; and his feeling for poetic prose was sound. Thus in his 1927 essay "On Re-reading the English Novelists," despite the limitations he found in the Brontës, he valued them above Thackeray because "they had a sense of beauty which heaven denied him." [87]

Almost twenty years earlier, upon reading Moore's *The Lake*, a work perhaps even more lyrical than narrative, he had remarked that it was "so smoothly written and so

[84] Hynes, *The Author's Craft*, p. 203.
[85] *Ibid.*, p. 207.
[86] *Books and Persons*, February 17, 1909.
[87] Hynes, *The Author's Craft*, p. 258.

calm and beautiful that I can enjoy reading it without even taking in the sense" (*Journal,* February 8, 1908). One could wish that more people had read *The Lake* precisely for the virtues Bennett praised. He also discovered new beauty upon rereading Moore's *A Mummer's Wife,* and certainly here he was thinking not of the total narrative structure, which may weary a modern reader, but of individual scenes regarded almost as separate poems. In his *Journal* for September 7, 1910, he noted that the book was "fine and beautiful. The Islington scenes are superb. You have squalor and sordidness turned into poetry. And the painter-like effects of visualization are splendid throughout."

Shortly after he had spoken in his *Journal* of the slightness of Conrad's *The Secret Agent* Bennett recorded his sensation of the novel as a whole. His comment still does not get at the theme of the book; but, with allowance for his delight in superlatives, it does describe the melancholy charm. He called it "a novel that is simply steeped in the finest beauty from end to end."[88] In Chekhov's stories Bennett found much the same lyric overtone. Writing of the two volumes *The Kiss* and *The Black Monk,* he asserted that in reading them "you will be drenched in the vast melancholy, savage and wistful, of Russian life; and you will have seen beauty."[89] And, of course, in the creation of melancholy beauty Turgenev was for Bennett, both early and late a master. Typical is his remark that Dostoevsky "could not compass the calm and exquisite soft beauty of 'On the Eve' or 'A House of Gentlefolk.'"[90]

The pocket philosophies were intended for the plain man and his wife, and so was Bennett's introduction to the study of literature, *Literary Taste: How to Form It* (1909).

[88] *Books and Persons,* May 8, 1908.
[89] *Ibid.,* March 18, 1909.
[90] *Ibid.,* March 31, 1910.

There are many sensible recommendations in the little book, but the best part is the analysis of Lamb's "Dream Children" for its theme, structure, and style. Bennett reveals the rigorous logic with which the fragile fantasy is kept from vanishing and the subtle variations in the language and rhythms as one mood gives way to another. Of all his own critical writing the pages on Lamb come the nearest to being poetic prose, and they are proof of the refinement of taste and feeling which Bennett possessed. It may be added that he might well have applied the same method to pages in the works of Henry James and Proust.

Of contemporary novelists the one who best gave Bennett what he wanted and needed was Thomas Hardy. It is not clear that in writing of the Five Towns Bennett thought of his task as comparable to Hardy's exploration of Wessex. But there is no question that, while learning from Moore and the French how to examine the day-by-day nature of the local scene, Bennett required poetic inspiration to lift his work above the commonplace, and an important source was Hardy. How early he first read his novels is unknown; in his *Journal*, January 6, 1900, he speaks familiarly of *A Few Crusted Characters*. During the succeeding years his admiration for Hardy increased. In "My Literary Heresies" he extolled *The Mayor of Casterbridge* for its originality: "It contains a new beauty, a new thrill for the amateurs of beauty."[91] Five years later, having again praised *The Mayor*, Bennett continued, "Never in English prose literature was such a seer of beauty as Thomas Hardy."[92]

In *The Author's Craft* (1914) he stressed the symbolism in the plot itself of *The Woodlanders* (59). In 1917, in his *Journal* he characterized *A Pair of Blue Eyes* as "full of fine

[91] Hynes, *The Author's Craft*, p. 239.
[92] *Books and Persons*, May 27, 1909.

things and immensely sardonic" (September 1). And in 1928, on rereading *Tess of the D'Urbervilles* he called it an "impressive masterpiece," and he regretted that in his *Evening Standard* article he had not put it "among Hardy's five best" (*Journal*, February 7). Newman Flower notes that Bennett considered *The Dynasts* "the greatest work written in our life-time." [93] In "On Re-reading the English Novelists" Bennett concluded by saying that he had "not discussed him who is conceivably the greatest of the Victorians. Of course I mean Thomas Hardy. He lives, and is thereby spared the infliction." [94] Bennett would have endorsed Hardy's views, and he could find his plots and characters interesting, but he would have been about as well pleased in these respects with other novelists. It was the impassioned poetry that made the difference.

Ultimately the beauty of a work of fiction for Bennett was inseparable from the author's imaginative compassion. There was beauty in tragic happenings only if the author had a feeling for the gentle sweetness of the suffering mortals whose mistakes and misfortunes he was depicting. In 1896, virtually at the outset of his career, Bennett set down in his *Journal* the dictum: "Essential characteristic of the really great novelist: a Christ-like, all-embracing compassion" (October 15). He found this, of course, in Hardy, who, to be sure, would not have characterized himself as being Christlike. He found it especially in Dostoevsky. Of the two early scenes in *Crime and Punishment* where the drunken Marmeladov laments his daughter's prostitution Bennett wrote, "They reach the highest and most terrible pathos that the novelist's art has ever reached." [95] Unlike Conrad, who could not endure Dostoevsky's "prehistoric mouthings," Bennett was

---

[93] Flower, *Just as It Happened*, p. 93.
[94] Hynes, *The Author's Craft*, p. 262.
[95] *Books and Persons*, March 31, 1910.

willing to immerse himself in the emotion with no
reservation—no fear lest what was naïve might also be
sentimental.

In *The Author's Craft* Bennett reiterated his belief that
to be great a novelist must have nobility of soul, and this
time it was Fielding, "unequalled among English novelists,"
who was his supreme example. To be sure, the argument
may somewhat beg the question, for Bennett certainly did
not approve of all the motives which in their private lives
had impelled his favorite authors. He was speaking of
them only as artists capable of escaping from their personal identities to live intensely in the sorrows and yearn-
ings of imaginary beings. If many others besides Hardy,
Dostoevsky, and Fielding could qualify, the antithesis for
Bennett was James Joyce. Though Bennett granted him
flashes of genius, he climaxed a devastating attack upon
him in "James Joyce's *Ulyssess*" with a most uncompas-
sionate pronouncement: "His vision of the world and its
inhabitants is mean, hostile, and uncharitable. He has a
colossal 'down' on humanity. Now Christ, in his all-
embracing charity, might have written a supreme novel.
Beelzebub could not." [96]

A corollary, perhaps, to his need for greatness of spirit
was the fact that a novelist must, above all, love his
principal character.[97] In *Point Counter Point* the essential
defect was that Huxley "hates and despises his characters." [98] Returning to Zola in *The Savour of Life*, Bennett
balanced praise with the complaint that Zola "lacked
sympathy," that he had a "chill, disillusioned hostility
towards human nature" (130). And one of several complaints against Galsworthy was that he insisted on drawing
his characters from the middle class, against which he had

[96] *Things That Have Interested Me (Second Series)*, pp. 198–199.
[97] *The Author's Craft*, p. 53.
[98] "The Progress of the Novel," in Hynes, *The Author's Craft*, p. 98.

a "fierce animosity." [99] In "The Progress of the Novel," where he tried to sum up the impressions of a lifetime, Bennett came back to his initial belief: "As a rule, but not always, the greatest novelists have been the greatest sympathisers." [100]

Even in 1929 the notion that creation of great literature required nobility of mind as well as mastery of the craft was becoming a little quaint. In some circles during the 1950's and 1960's it was to be dismissed as naïve. Indeed, with all his alertness to new ways, Bennett remained in a tradition that included Fielding, Scott, Meredith, and Hardy. However pertinent to man as a social being, literature, for Bennett, was not a device for political or social renovation; still less was it a means for publicly exhibiting whatever violent feelings might be at war in an author's soul. Bennett's concern was human nature, not the peculiarity of a unique nature; and he expected an author to meditate the overwhelming passions, the irresistible impulses toward violent action, until he had acquired some confidence that he comprehended them and could depict them in an orderly way. He also believed that, however sordid his subject matter, an author should focus on its inherent aspects of beauty.

A writer's mastery of the stuff of life which he used and his attitude toward it would be revealed in his tone, for the tone of a work of literature expressed the author's dominant feeling toward all the welter of existence which he sought to comprehend. Consequently, among the hundreds of casual allusions to literature in the *Journal* the most common notation has to do, directly or obliquely, with the tone. If an author possessed nobility of mind and a sensitivity to beauty, the evidence was to be found, as in Lamb's "Dream Children," in the tone. On rereading ⌐⌐

[99] "The Novel-Reading Public," in *ibid.*, p. 79.
[100] *Ibid.*, p. 95.

Rouge et le Noire, for example, Bennett was struck both with its truthfulness and its "grand manner" (*Journal,* February 14, 1910). Some ten years later, when recording his admiration of *La Chartreuse de Parme,* he spoke of "the wit, the power, the variety, the grace, the naturalness, and the continuous distinction of this book" (*Journal,* August 2, 1920). Both comments say, in effect, that Stendhal's tone conveys a significant view of reality.

Despite the handicap of translation Bennett sensed in their depiction of emotion the fine quality of the great Russians; and it was Turgenev and Chekhov, who wrote with melancholy grace, to whom Bennett, in his own reflective moments, was most attuned. He liked their quiet manner and their wistful acceptance of the sadness inherent in mortality. In *Fame and Fiction* he compared Turgenev's works to an "antique statue," and he remarked that "their beauty, instead of delivering a blow, steals towards you and mildly penetrates the frame" (226). He mentioned Turgenev's intense "Oriental melancholy," and called him, at the same time, an "evangel of vague and quiescent hope, with dreamy eyes upon the furthest future" (228).

When he read either essays or fiction Bennett tried to immerse himself directly in the emotion through the style itself. It was this habit to which he referred in saying that he could enjoy *The Lake* "without even taking in the sense." Naturally, of course, he really did not divorce sound and sense. But as he read such diverse authors as Isaiah, Sir Thomas Browne, Ruskin, Stevenson, and James Russell Lowell he found his own mood and attitude shaped by the tone of their work, even as it was by that of Marcus Aurelius.[101] It was the severity of Gibbon's *Decline and Fall of the Roman Empire* that attracted him—the dramatic

[101] Cf. *Literary Taste,* p. 31; *Journal,* January 13, 1904; *Your United States,* p. 63.

tenseness and the restrained fire.[102] In Gogol's *Dead Souls*
it was the "sardonic humour."[103] And long before the
adjective-noun "absurd" had become a shibboleth
Bennett aptly characterized the tone of much of Hardy's
irony by saying that Hardy viewed the earth as a "won-
drous, lovely, disconcerting jocularity on the part of an
Unknowable with sardonic leanings towards the absurd."[104]

As to the structure of a novel, Bennett seemed to feel
that, except for some obvious matters, it was virtually a
thing of instinct. In *The Author's Craft* he asserted that,
except for Turgenev, "the great novelists of the world,
according to my own standards, have either ignored
technique or have failed to understand it" (48). He was,
of course, overlooking James and seriously underrating a
number of others; in fact, he went on to depreciate his
earlier masters Flaubert and Maupassant despite their
being "exceptional artists." In contrast, he called Balzac
a "prodigious blunderer" and Stendhal a scorner of
technique; and he wound up his rhetorical outburst,
". . . what a hasty, amorphous lump of gold is the sublime,
the unapproachable *Brothers Karamazov!*" He could, however, speak of Turgenev's excellent economy, and he could
pronounce Chekhov "unequalled in the technique of the
short story," his only rival being Conrad.[105] He could
even admire Dumas's narrative skill in *The Queen's Necklace.*

Most of his comments on technique are complaints
rather than commendations, and they are not based on
any formula concerning structure. Instead, they reflect
Bennett's feeling that here or there the theme or mood of a
work suffered from slighted execution. This was his ob-
jection to both *Bel Ami* and *Une Vie* (*Journal*, November 17,

[102] *Literary Taste*, pp. 29–30.
[103] Hynes, *The Author's Craft*, p. 117.
[104] "The Novels of Eden Phillpotts," in *ibid.*, p. 179.
[105] Hynes, *ibid.*, pp. 118, 120.

1903, and March 28, 1908). It underlay his annoyance with *Anna Karenina*, which was "not one novel but two," and his strictures on both *War and Peace* and Meredith's *Rhoda Fleming*, which he felt lacked centers.[106] Conrad's *Lord Jim* was good despite its "clumsy machinery."[107] *The Shadow Line* was also good, but had "a certain anti-climax where the climax ought to be" (*Journal*, March 23, 1917). Lawrence's *The Lost Girl* was "fine," but could be "great if it had a clear central theme and comprehensible construction" (*Journal*, November 30, 1920). Even Virginia Woolf's *To the Lighthouse* had some good things in it, but the devices for marking the passing of time were unsuccessful.[108] Perhaps the most apt of Bennett's complaints about technique concerns not a novel, but Strindberg's *The Father*, which he pronounced to be the "work of a madman, inconsequent, loose, too quick, too slow, sort of shaking all the time" (*Journal*, September 2, 1927).

Bennett's usual way of approaching a novel was to try to get a feeling for it in its entirety—albeit too often from a reading that was too much a mere scansion—and then to sample scenes and passages. Thus he could notice how the French realists and Moore built up their evidence in a given scene; and turning to so different an author as Mrs. Humphry Ward, he could approve, though not wish to emulate, the realism she achieved "by dint of laborious and carefully ordered detail" (*Journal*, September 29, 1896). So it was that he could speak of *Nana* as a "tremendous achievement of colossal and dignified labour" (*Journal*, February 21, 1904), and similarly admire the extensive use of detail in *Crime and Punishment* (*Journal*, June 11, 1910).

[106] *The Author's Craft*, p. 54.
[107] *Books and Persons*, July 11, 1908.
[108] "Virginia Woolf's *To the Lighthouse*," in Hynes, *The Author's Craft*, p. 221, and *The Savour of Life*, p. 312.

Before he decided to limit his respect for James, Bennett bemoaned the carelessness that annoyed him in too many novels and, in contrast, he found James to be "flawless" (*Journal*, December 21, 1897). About the same time he acclaimed the "meticulous care" in the style of Ross and Somerville's *The Silver Fox* and concluded his entry with the remark that only in Pater and James "can it be said that the choice and position of *every* word and stop has been the subject of separate consideration" (*Journal*, February 1, 1898). Using the same standard he unhesitatingly chided Wells and, later, Walpole for their loose, careless writing.

In appreciating the style of Turgenev, Bennett was, of course, restrained by the obstacle of translation. His favorite stylist among novelists who wrote in English was perhaps Hawthorne. In *The Savour of Life* he remarked that George Moore revealed to him that "no finer prose than Hawthorne's was written in the nineteenth century" (134). Pages later, while struggling with the wretched style of *An American Tragedy*, he took occasion to cite Hawthorne as "a writer of some of the loveliest English ever printed" (304). The works of Hawthorne and Turgenev—and Lamb—do not directly remind one of *Clayhanger* or *Riceyman Steps*, and they are remote indeed from *Buried Alive* or *Mr. Prohack*. But their quiet charm and pensive melancholy gave solace and inspiration to Bennett. They endured.

CHAPTER FOUR

The Practice of the Craft

WHAT BENNETT SAID about other men's fiction was a
mirror, albeit sometimes cloudy, of the intent and methods
of his own. As we have seen, he had no interest in the
history of literary theory. His allusions to critics are usually
casual, and those he mentions are most commonly concerned with the philosophic or inspirational nature of
literature rather than with the art. In *Fame and Fiction*
(1901) he revealed some acquaintance with Goethe's
views on what gave distinction to a work of literature, and
in his *Journal* in 1905 he spoke of rereading *Wilhelm
Meister*. Some two years later he noted having read in
Lessing's *Laocoön* "to taste for a change the philosophy of
art" (*Journal*, September 25, 1907), and in *Books and
Persons* he briefly praised Lessing as "somebody who knows
what he is talking about . . . someone who has been there"
(October 21, 1909). In the same work he was enthusiastic
about Lamb's "taste and his powerful intelligence" (October 27, 1910). In 1916 he wrote George Doran that he
liked Stuart Pratt Sherman's article on Bennett himself—
a typical Sherman essay, concerned with moral and
spiritual values in Bennett's novels.[1]

[1] Letter dated May 2, 1916 (*Letters*, III, 11). Sherman's article, "The
Realism of Arnold Bennett," first appeared in the *Nation*.

These few scattered allusions and others equally fragmentary attest to Bennett's preoccupation with what makes
an inspiring narrative work. In praising Paul Hervieu's *Le
Dédale*, for example, he summed up the effect of its three
middle acts: "Constant spiritual action of the piece, and
constant drama, conflict of emotions, etc., rising at times
to great heights" (*Journal*, March 23, 1904). Put in a
different way, this was the concept of fiction expressed in
a significant passage in the *Journal* while Bennett was at
work on *The Old Wives' Tale*. After complaining that some
novels of "sexual sentimentality" he had been reading
lacked "nobility," that they did not "arouse a single really
fine emotion," he continued: "That is what there has got
to be in *The Old Wives' Tale*—a lofty nobility. I got it now
and then in *Whom God Hath Joined*, but in the next book
I must immensely increase the dose" (*Journal*, July 22,
1907).

Earlier, in *How to Become an Author*, he had remarked
that a writer "must 'work himself up' at the start," and
that he must sustain a "lofty plane of emotional excitement" (130). For his own inspiration, as we have noticed,
Bennett liked to hear good music or to read poetry. Near
the end of his career, after noting that he ordinarily
preferred prose to verse, he added:

> When I read classical poetry [which included Shake-
> speare's plays] I do so for an ulterior purpose—because
> I find that if I am writing a novel or story, the finest
> English verse has the capacity to lift me up out of the rut
> of composition and set me, and my work, on a higher
> plane.[2]

In 1929 Bennett found himself in a "fever of apprehension" about *The Imperial Palace*, which he had not yet

---

[2] *Journal 1929*, n.d., p. 159.

begun to put on paper. At the opera, during a selection from Rimsky-Korsakov's *Sadko*, he lost himself in meditation of his new work, and soon afterward he wrote in his *Journal*: ". . . as soon as I was outside the theatre I knew I had got hold of the affair, because everything that caught my attention related itself to the novel, gave me fresh notions for the novel." His entry continues: "A novel in process of creation has to be lifted up. It may have to be lifted up again and again. . . . To work this miracle there is nothing as efficacious as the sight or hearing of a great work of art—any art." [3] To the inspiration of the arts must be added the quieter, but pervasive influence of Marcus Aurelius and perhaps of Herbert Spencer, of whose influence Bennett wrote, "You can see *First Principles* in nearly every line I write" (*Journal*, September 15, 1910).

In short, Bennett approached serious writing of fiction essentially like a poet. The emotional tone came first. Implied in meditation upon the passions, which were the substance, was an inevitable concern for theme. Only after the lyric nature of the work had been determined was Bennett concerned with the craft. And though in the rather glib *How to Become an Author* he did enunciate some obvious principles and also recommended John Nichol's *English Composition*, he had no formulas. His own works derived their special craftsmanship from his study of the methods of others and from his attempt to fuse two points of view—the realistic and the romantic.

To say that Bennett invariably sensed in his material a universal theme or parable is not to mean that he set out to preach or even necessarily to explore a specific idea. In "The Progress of the Novel" (1929), he enunciated as a basic principle: "A novelist should be interested first in people. When his interest in an idea gets the better of his interest in people, the idea lays a curse upon his art.

[3] *Ibid.*, August 28.

('Ideas are the curse of art,' said Edmond de Goncourt, too loosely)."[4] Actually, for Bennett the plight of human beings inevitably suggested themes. In 1896, for example, after viewing the portraits of celebrities at the Royal Academy and admitting that they probably had little artistic merit, he continued: "To study these faces of men and women brings one in contact with activities, ideals, ambitions . . . " (*Journal*, April 30). It was about thirty-two years later that he found in the lifelike statue of a woman in the National Museum in Athens the suggestion of the fascinating ambivalent relationship of the sexes.[5] Meanwhile the sight of the crotchety woman at the Parisian Duval had led to the story of the transformation of two young, vivacious girls into two middle-aged and then two old women. The theme was there in the character, and with it came a feeling for the tone; the plot remained to be invented.

Upon reading Shorter's *Charlotte Brontë and Her Circle* Bennett jotted down the possibility of a novel with the heroine possessed of the "sombre splendours of Emily's character" (*Journal*, November 5, 1896). He never wrote that story, but the motif hints of his method, the distilling of a trait or two and omitting the rest. In *The Author's Craft* he recorded some of the types of character which Balzac "brazenly" and successfully repeated (63). He himself in his portraits, especially those of women, was to feel equally free to repeat himself. In fact, in a letter to Frank Harris, December 13, 1908, he called Critchlow of *The Old Wives' Tale* "*my* character," who "keeps recurring (under different names with slight changes) in my stuff."[6] In 1924 Bennett referred to a recent discussion with T. S. Eliot on characterization, the gist being that "a character

---

[4] Hynes, *The Author's Craft*, p. 90.
[5] *Mediterranean Scenes*, p. 57.
[6] *Letters*, II, 245.

has to be conventionalized" (*Journal*, September 11, 1924).
Only then, he felt, would he impress the reader and live
on in his memory. It was with this concept of the character
as expressive of a dominant theme or exhibiting one attitude toward life that he could write, "The foundation of
good fiction is character-creating and nothing else."[7]

So much for theory. But characters did not spring into
being with magic swiftness; they evolved. To be sure, the
broad delineations—the conventionalizations—were obvious enough, even as with any stock creations; and the
notes on the principal characters in *Flora*, acted in 1927,[8]
are probably typical of Bennett's methods for the thirty
previous years. There are persons like Lucian, Flora, and
their daughter Clare in various earlier Bennett stories and
plays, especially the lighter ones.

The note on Lucian reads: "About 50. Good-looking.
Slightly dandiacal. A martyr, an egotist, but generally
charming, and always urbane. So smooth that there is
nothing to catch hold of." With so general a sketch one
could fill in the lineaments of a number of middle-aged
characters, most notably perhaps Mr. Prohack. With a
slight, but significant variation from his predecessors
Lucian becomes the husband who has added no romance
to his wife's existence and who typifies the dread bleakness
of a culturally sterile middle age.

Flora has lived in Bennett stories since the days of
Leonora: "Just under 40. Slim. Handsome. Nervous, but
dignified. Reserved. Her deportment and tones show
capability. She cannot but inspire respect; but to inspire
devotion, she needs knowing." The challenge to the author,
of course, was to make her worth knowing. As fifty had
become the crucial age for Bennett's men, when they
were either to display a romantic boyishness or decline

[7] *Things That Have Interested Me: Third Series*, p. 161.
[8] Published in *Five Three-Act Plays* (London: Rich and Cowan, 1933).

into unromantic dullness, "just under 40" was the poignant time for a spirited, attractive woman. Even the pocket
philosophies discuss her type.

As for Clare, her sisters and cousins, now and then a
little older, often playfully amusing, have also been wandering through Bennett's scenes. Most often they have
been in the fantasias and next often in the light romances,
such as *Mr. Prohack*, and one of them, Pearl, will make her
appearance in *Accident*. An early avatar is Helen in *Helen
with the High Hand* (1910), who takes over her great-
uncle's home and magnanimously becomes his tyrant.
Clare's description reads: "20. Developing from the hoy-
den into the young lady. Highly interested in her own
development, especially in her new power over men. A
rough wit; chiefly pert, full of charm. Adores and pities
her mother. Adores and defies her father." Bennett very
early fell in love with the type—not seriously, to be sure,
as it was the Leonora's and Flora's who had mature charm
and were worthy of exalted romance.

Given their broad lineaments, Lucian, Flora, and Clare
must, of course, as quickly as possible reveal an individuality of their own; so that Lucian is discovered to be by
no means Mr. Prohack, Flora shows a courage well beyond Leonora's, and Clare becomes a moral rebel. It is
both their impulses and the circumstances of their lives
which bring about the universality of their appeal and the
uniqueness of their given cases. For Bennett the circumstances were very important indeed. It is, in fact, the part
they play that leads us to the portrait of Mrs. Brown; for it
is in the controversy between Bennett and Virginia Woolf
over how Bennett, among others, would make us acquainted
with this imaginary woman that we can best approach his
methods of characterization.

Bennett's strictures on Mrs. Woolf appeared mainly
after her attacks upon him in 1923 and 1924, but since

by implication they justify the very methods which Mrs. Woolf caricatured, we shall consider them first. Though he credited Mrs. Woolf with originality, he wrote of *Jacob's Room*, "But the characters do not vitally survive in the mind, because the author has been obsessed by details of originality and cleverness."[9] He brought much the same charge against *Mrs. Dalloway:* "Mrs. Woolf (in my opinion) told us ten thousand things about Mrs. Dalloway but did not show us Mrs. Dalloway."[10] In fact, Bennett complained that in the work of all the new school of which Mrs. Woolf was the leader the characters did not "sufficiently live." Her own method was, of course, to let the characters through dialogue give glimpses of the thoughts and impressions with which they were pre-occupied. Her reader may feel, however, that, though he knows what the thoughts are, he is not very sure as to the personality of a character, and he may have little notion as to what to expect of him from one scene to another. It is not really the technique that is in question, for in James's *The Awkward Age* we come to know the characters very well though we have only their scraps of dialogue to tell us who they really are. What bothered Bennett was that he could not construct a human being from the separate fragments which Mrs. Woolf provided.

Mrs. Woolf on her part insisted that Bennett never entered the minds of his characters, that, indeed, he gave only the incidental external trappings of their existence. Now the possible injustice of Bennett to Mrs. Woolf does not concern us, but hers to Bennett does.[11] For Bennett consciously did what she accused him of, but

[9] *Things That Have Interested Me: Third Series*, p. 162.
[10] *The Savour of Life*, p. 58.
[11] In "Mr. Bennett and Mrs. Woolf," *Modern Fiction Studies*, VIII (1962), 103–115, Irving Kreuz remarks, "If Mrs. Woolf's is a misreading of Bennett's novel, his is a *non*-reading of hers."

not in the irrelevant manner of her *reductio ad absurdum* portrayal of Mrs. Brown.[12]

Bennett was for Mrs. Woolf a major exemplar of a narrative method which she and her associates were rejecting. To illustrate her point she imagined a Mrs. Brown in a railway carriage. She filled in the main lineaments as any spectator would presumably see them. Mrs. Brown "was poorly dressed and very small. She had an anxious, harassed look. I doubt whether she was what you call an educated woman."[13] After a quick summary of how Wells and Galsworthy, like Bennett out-of-date as to literary technique, would fill in the portrait, she turned to Bennett:

> Mr. Bennett, alone of the Edwardians, would keep his eyes in the carriage. He, indeed, would observe every detail with immense care. He would notice the advertisements; the pictures of Swanage and Portsmouth; the way in which the cushion bulged between the buttons; how Mrs. Brown wore a brooch which had cost three-and-ten-three at Whitworth's bazaar; and had mended both gloves—indeed the thumb of the left-hand glove had been replaced. And he would observe, at length, how this was the non-stop train from Windsor which calls at Richmond for the convenience of middle-class residents . . . . And so he would gradually sidle sedately towards Mrs. Brown, and would remark how she had been left a little copyhold, not freehold property at Datchet, which, however, was mortgaged to Mr. Bungay the solicitor. (100–101)

[12] For the first version of Mrs. Woolf's "Mr. Bennett and Mrs. Brown," printed in *Nation and Atheneum*, XXXIV (December 1, 1923), 342–343, cf. Hynes, *The Author's Craft*, pp. 269–273. The version which she read to "The Heretics," at Cambridge, May 18, 1924, is in *The Captain's Death Bed* (London: The Hogarth Press, 1950), pp. 90–111.

[13] *The Captain's Death Bed*, p. 100.

Insisting that her imitation was authentic, Mrs. Woolf proceeded to quote from the portrait of Hilda in *Hilda Lessways*. She approved of Bennett's introductory details showing Hilda's concern for her mother and her intensity of feeling; but then, she maintained, Bennett rather forgot Hilda while describing the neighborhood. She quoted his allusions to the Turnhill canal, the flour mill, the kilns, and the new cottages, from among which Hilda expected the rent collector to emerge. Against all these external paraphernalia Mrs. Woolf protested, "One line of insight would have done more than all those lines of description . . . . And now—where is Hilda?" Her answer was, of course, that the restless girl was "still looking out of the window," and so she continued with Bennett's description of what Hilda saw:

> The row was called Freehold Villas: a consciously proud name in a district where much of the land was copyhold . . . . Most of the dwellings were owned by their occupiers, who, each an absolute monarch of the soil, niggled in his sooty garden of an evening amid the flutter of drying shirts and towels. Freehold Villas symbolized the final triumph of Victorian economics, the apotheosis of the prudent and industrious artisan . . . . And indeed it was a very real achievement. Nevertheless, Hilda's irrational contempt would not admit this. (102)

This is, of course, not the end. Having, according to Mrs. Woolf, promised at last to go on with Hilda, Bennett turns instead to a long paragraph on the four houses of which Hilda and her mother occupied one, and, after speaking of the rates and the history of the dwellings, winds up: "It was admittedly the best row of houses in that newly-settled quarter of the town. In coming to it out of Freehold Villas Mr. Skellorn obviously came to something superior, wider, more liberal. Suddenly Hilda heard her mother's voice . . . " (103).

One can begin by saying that in her attempt at a parody Mrs. Woolf was much more obtuse than Bennett ever was in his demurrers on James or Proust. In short, she was accusing Bennett of wasting her time. What she was refusing to see was his purpose behind the not really overlong description of the neighborhood. It should be stated, to begin with, that Bennett did not invariably proceed as here with Hilda, but since he did something rather similar in fitting into their Five-Towns environment Anna Tellwright, the Baines sisters, and Clayhanger, his intent is indeed pertinent.

First of all, he wanted to create a striking character. That character, however, was not to spring forth from a vacuum with a set of thoughts and feelings which would be released to the reader a little at a time in bits of dialogue or stream-of-consciousness reflections. The character, instead, was to be seen in relief against a background which would provide a basis for interpretation. It was not just that Hilda was restive, even rebellious. She was restive in a lower middle-class home possessing comforts which, though not substantial, represented Victorian material progress. Hers was a proud neighborhood, even though every day of her life Hilda had been conscious of sooty gardens and drying shirts and towels.

To be sure, Bennett could have given a rapid notation of her idle thoughts in which some of the external phenomena would have been enumerated. He merely found it simpler and more natural to choose the pertinent details and record them objectively. Granted that he did not say at the moment just why they were relevant. But as the story unfolds and Hilda appears in other scenes, the reader should still remember the street upon which she looks and perceive that her rebellion is not an unrestricted casting off of Victorian trammels. The child has been mother to the woman, and Hilda carries with her all the inhibitions, all the cultural limitations, all the Victorian materialism which have imprinted themselves upon her youthful consciousness.

This is another way of saying that, without writing a deterministic story in which a character is the helpless victim of his environment and the accidents which confront and destroy him, Bennett nevertheless saw the world in which a character grew up as an indelible influence on his nature and view of life. Anna, as his title explicitly stated, was of the Five Towns, more specifically of that part in which a Tellwright could be expected to live. Hilda was of the northernmost of the Five Towns, within which there were social gradations of a subtle precision. The Baines sisters were not just from the Five Towns, but from Bursley, and not from some nondescript section, but from the corner of St. Luke's Square. And they were all Victorian maidens, whether gratefully or resentfully.

In short, whatever may have been the immediate hint, as in the seeing of the *maniaque* in the Duval, the heroines really came into being for Bennett as an expression of some aspect of the social world which he best knew. In this sense St. Luke's Square had a history and part of that history was revealed through the lives of Constance and Sophia Baines.

Now, what Mrs. Woolf did not touch upon was the relation of what she quoted to Bennett's theme. The important fact, of course, is that at one and the same moment Bennett was trying to accumulate details which would culminate in a character portrait that his reader would remember, to interpret the immediate past as he personally sensed its lingering effects, and to say something about the great longings, the passions, inherent in mortal existence. Everything he says about Hilda's street and dwelling place, either in Turnhill or later in Brighton, and about her own sensations of them also says something about the human struggle to find freedom, about the bitterness and the resilience of youth, or perhaps about the pathos of aging and defeat.

These were among Bennett's perennial themes, and it is because so many of his heroines confront the same problems that, with all their individuality, they are, like Balzac's, of a sisterhood. When Bennett saw the *maniaque* he at once thought not merely of a story with an old woman as chief character, but of the pathos of a young woman's growing old. So the theme was concomitant with the conception of the character. And it perhaps goes without saying that the theme brought with it the tone.

As for plot, though Bennett once remarked that it was the "primary thing in fiction,"[14] and at another time asserted, "Lord, give us plot,"[15] he expected a novel's major outlines to be shaped by the theme. The details were, of course, another matter. They must be in harmony with the total plan, but the author must be free to fit into his story particular impressions which especially struck him, even those that came to him at any casual moment as he was working his way through a chapter.

Ultimately it was not the over-all structure that distinguished a good novel from a bad one; it was the quality of each scene, each sentence. And thinking always of art as a revelation of life, Bennett was concerned therefore with the quality of life which he could make concrete in his fictional world. This meant that he must, first of all, be alert to the world around him to pick up sensations which might have unusual significance. Hence the justification for putting away somewhere in his mind, if not on the pages of his *Journal*, anecdotes and images that would serve as touchstones or as the actual substance of his fiction. We have already noted his remark that at the funeral

[14] *How to Become an Author*, p. 92.
[15] Hynes, *The Author's Craft*, p. 72.

of Willie Boulton he might well have imitated the Goncourts by recording his sensations.

When put into a narrative one's impressions might illu-
minate a character and they must in some way support
the theme; but, first of all, they had validity in their own
right, just as much so in a novel as in a journal consisting
of impressions almost exclusively. Now, it is true that
many of the impressions in Bennett's fiction are of the
kind which Mrs. Woolf would find superficial and irrelevant. Some are of the material aspects of life—the physical
comforts, the marks of success, the external trappings
which identify a square in Bursley or a row of houses in
Turnhill or Bleakridge. But for Bennett they had integrity.
Though in so far as he was a romantic he could speculate
on the longings in the mind of a Leonora or a Hilda
Lessways, he still needed the circumstantial evidence to
support his convictions. To guess what preoccupied others
Bennett had first to determine what in St. John's Square
or in Clerkenwell struck his own imagination and cheered
or depressed him, and to gather from anecdotes hints as to
primary human motives. Having made up his own mind
on matters which might in a way be abstractly summarized, he must again render them concrete in the
telling.

When Bennett fell short, it was not because he told what
Hilda's window looked out upon. It was because he had
not made his images sufficiently fresh and concrete.
Instead of putting together a stained glass made up of
brilliant bits of blue, green, yellow, and other single
colors, he had settled for the general effect which these
should produce and in so doing had sacrificed intensity
and freshness. It may be stated in all fairness that he was
not the only significant writer to let stand descriptions
that were without distinction. Even a stream-of-consciousness technique is no assurance against flatness.

But to recognize the limitations in execution is a rather simple negative matter. What is of much more interest is the fact that success is a most evasive thing and that throughout his career Bennett was trying to improve. Study of the methods of the Goncourts or of Balzac's way of building up the social atmosphere in *Ursule Mirouet* or *Le Médecin de Campagne* revealed only what others had been able to do. To be original Bennett had to trust his own eyes and ears, and the *Journal* is a vast compendium of the raw material which he found.

At the outset Bennett set down the principle he should follow. Obviously thinking of his French masters, he wrote in his *Journal* in 1897, "The novelist of contemporary manners needs to be saturated with a sense of the picturesque in modern things" (January 11). To illustrate his precept he noted things he had observed during a walk in King's Road in a "grey fog." There was a "mysterious beauty" in the houses and barren trees and everything was "curiously strange and novel and wonderful." He concluded his entry: "The novelist should cherish and burnish this faculty of seeing crudely, simply, artlessly, ignorantly; of seeing like a baby or a lunatic, who lives each moment by itself and tarnishes the present by no remembrance of the past." [16] In short, one must not destroy the vividness of an image or incident by sentimental rumination. This did not, of course, mean indifference to its thematic implications.

What particularly set Bennett's inventiveness to work was witnessing or learning of an incident or circumstance that might startlingly reveal character or suggest a story about the human predicament. Thus, upon reading Moore's *Evelyn Innes*, he was struck with the possibility of a work on the triumphal career of a prima donna. At once he

---

[16] In *A Man from the North*, Mr. Aked recommends as a nightly exercise the writing of six hundred words about something seen during the day.

thought of how he could get authentic material by perhaps having tea with one. Immediately, however, he was haunted by one of his favorite themes, and so he added, "The old age of the prima donna and her death might make a superbly cruel contrast to the rest of the story— astringent, chilling, unbearably hopeless, and bitter with reminiscence" (*Journal*, June 9, 1898).

It was a few months later that he recorded the wistfulness of the barmaid's face as she gazed at Adeline Genée, only, minutes later, to treat her own admirers with the same casual aplomb as did her idol. He described the event with childlike simplicity, but he also sensed the story in it. He was always intrigued by tales of eccentrics. In 1907 he was told the bizarre story of a man's obsessive, doting tyranny over his wife (*Journal*, August 1, 1907). Some years later he transformed it into one of his light romances, "Middle-Aged." He was drawn especially by the antics of misers; a *Journal* entry of October 20, 1907, on an old woman miser living expensively in Paris while saving on light and mutton found its way into "The Tight Hand" and obliquely into *Riceyman Steps*.

Having transmuted the incident at the Duval into the narrative of two sisters' growing old and dying, and having decided to give one of the girls a sojourn in Paris, Bennett needed authentic details about life during the occupation of 1870 and the Commune. When he talked about the events with his landlord and his wife, who had lived through the events of 1870, he was impressed with their casualness in speaking of the shooting in the streets (*Journal*, November 19, 1907). Here was a crude, simple, artless account on the basis of which he could build the tenor of life for Sophia as the melodramatic and pathological came to be for her and her tenants the ordinary and natural.

Writing to his brother Septimus, June 14, 1917, Bennett

spoke of Marguerite's having been in a train that was hit
by a bomb, and he indicated that he had examined her as
to what happened. *The Pretty Lady* may have incorporated
some of her impressions and reactions; for it, like *The Old
Wives' Tale*, is concerned with shock and adjustment during wartime, and the subject of one scene is a bombing of
London. Bennett's involvement in a railroad accident, as
we have noted, became transformed many years later into
a major scene in his light novel *Accident*. These are among
hundreds of incidents recorded by Bennett which suggested motifs for the action in a fictional scene or might
serve as touchstones for describing a character's sensations.
Few were directly used, but the tone and implication of
dozens of others permeate the novels.

If the personal anecdote hinted of the generic qualities
and emotions of mankind, the scenes that fed the eye as
one strolled in Paris, London, or the Five Towns were also
suggestive, for they attested to the values and aspirations
of civilized man. In observing the scene before him Bennett
could cherish individual details, but in the main he looked
as an impressionist. It was magnitude and tone that
mattered, even as in an impressionistic painting. The
principle which dominated his artistic career he set down
early in the *Journal*. June 15, 1897, he strolled through the
West End among crowds of sightseers and workmen preparing for the Jubilee. After an enumeration of a mixture
of details and impressions—on women's frocks, the tops of
buses, carpenters in their aprons, drivers in "grey felt
hats," and "vehicles six and eight deep"—he ended with
an especially impressionistic sentence: "In all the gutters
poles springing up, decorated with muslins and streamers
and gilt apexes, and here and there patches daily growing
bigger, of red and blue draperies covering the yellow wood
of jubilee stands." Having carried out his maxim of some
five months earlier to saturate himself in the picturesque

and to observe naïvely, he now went on to a generalization: "Everything, taken separately, ugly and crude, yet in combination, by sheer immensity and bold crudity, certain in the end to produce a great spectacular effect."

It was during the following September that, after alluding to his description of the potteries in the introduction to *Anna Tellwright* (*Anna of the Five Towns*), he wrote a long paragraph on the impressions of Burslem gleaned on "early morning walks." Included in the midst of his notation of what his eyes surveyed was the remark "It is *not* beautiful in detail, but its smoke transforms its ugliness into a beauty transcending the work of architects and of time" (*Journal*, September 10, 1897).[17]

Some ten years later on a December day Bennett again walked among the potteries. This time he again enumerated details, but his concern was once more for the over-all impression—of a cold "clammy" Sunday morning, with "men in bright neckties sallying forth," each presenting a "rather suspicious, defiant, meanly shrewd look," and with the "sound of hymns from chapels and schools" (*Journal*, December 22, 1907). Here were the images and the tone which would undergo no great transformation in such works as *Clayhanger* during the next two decades.[18] It was the same approach to Clerkenwell that made possible the impressionistic selection of detail in *Riceyman Steps*.

Whether beautiful or ugly, such scenes interested Bennett both as a realist and as a romantic. And he always looked beyond the immediate scene to all the hidden elements which revealed man's genius and the miracle of civilization.

[17] Cf. also a similar description of Green Park and the Strand during an October walk in the mist and fog (*Journal*, October 6, 1897).

[18] October 20, 1927, Bennett rode through the Potteries on the train and noted laconically in his *Journal*, "The sight of this district gave me a shudder."

In "The Fallow Fields of Fiction" (1901), Bennett suggested topics worthy of exploration in a novel. One was the building of Westminster cathedral, the narration of which would "comprise a large segment of the circle of life; it might include all passions, and many various activities both artistic and commercial. It would be dramatic, and certainly it would be realistic. Finally it would be grandiose, and would culminate in a spectacle of sheer beauty." [19] He sketched a few items to be incorporated in such a novel. Twenty-nine years later he was to perform a somewhat comparable task in *The Imperial Palace*, for which he was to proceed systematically in collecting both precise details and generic impressions.

In the same essay he demonstrated the romance of the railway system as it was epitomized in the Scottish express. He began with a woman proud to be the wife of a Paddington ticket seller, went on to the engineer "in blue, with a bowler-hat" about to step self-importantly into the cabin of the express, and ended with a porter discussing the directors of the company. He also found the "corporate life" of a community an excellent subject for a novel, and it was a few years later that he called the very creation of electricity out of Burslem "refuse" "one of those slightly sentimental, morally spectacular aspects of municipal life that *do* impress."

Neither Bennett's methods nor the intent behind them would have interested Virginia Woolf. Indeed, by 1924 they might easily be labeled traditional. But they had honorable antecedents, most notably in *La Comédie Humaine*. And if they did not represent innovation in literary art, they were still relevant in the concept of the novel as a branch of the humanities, for Bennett saw himself as a cultural historian as well as an interpreter of the individual human consciousness, and his province was

[19] Hynes, *The Author's Craft*, p. 69.

from the middle 1860's, or even earlier, to the 1920's. His record, however incomplete and limited by his own personal experience, was that of an acutely sensitive mind. For that matter, it also had its own literary merit, as we shall see.

Much of what we have been discussing concerns Bennett as artist seeing the novel as a means of revealing beauty and truth; but the art depended upon mastery of the craft. There are a number of comments in the nonfiction and even occasional allusions in the fiction itself which remind us that, as a craftsman, Bennett was a disciple of Balzac, Moore, the Goncourts, Flaubert, and Maupassant. Actually, he gleaned hints from widely diverse writers. In *A Man from the North* the hero, Larch, who aspires to authorship, studies a Maupassant story for its technique, but in trying to write about London he finds his narrative "distinctly resembled" Stevenson's *New Arabian Nights*. Bennett himself was, of course, really attempting the novel he ascribed to Larch. The fusion of Maupassant and Stevenson to the extent that it was successful represented a blending of realism and romance.

In 1908 while reading Stendhal and the Paul Léautaud preface to selections from him, Bennett recognized the effectiveness of Stendhal's "hastiness of style; never going back etc., 'getting the stuff down' (as I say) without affectation or pose." Though he could "quite see the weakness of the argument," he noted: "Yet so influenced by what he says that I at once began to do my novel [*The Old Wives' Tale*] more *currente calamo!* Sentences without verbs, etc. See chapters in Part II, birth of baby and kids' party, etc." (*Journal*, April 3). The device had a certain value for impressionism. The next year he remarked in his *Journal*, "More and more struck with Chekhov, and more and more inclined to write a lot of very short stories in the same technique" (February 26, 1909). He added that, though written before he had read Chekhov, "The Death of Simon Fuge" was "in the same technique and about as good. Though to say anything is as good as *Ward No. 6* in *The Black Monk* wants a bit of nerve."

In 1920, some six years before *Lord Raingo* appeared, with its detailed deathbed scene, Bennett was thinking of a novel based on the old age of Beaverbrook's father. In his *Journal* he noted: "I read *Le Curé de Campagne* for the death-bed scene at the end. I shall have a great death-bed scene at the end of my novel, and I want to stage it with the utmost magnificence. I got a tip or two from Balzac, but he is not at his best in this book and can be bettered" (March 9). In *The Imperial Palace* Bennett returned to the Goncourts for "the episode of the gloves, . . . which I found in and appropriated from the *Journal* of the brothers de Goncourt."[20] For his lighter novels and plays he drew upon Wilkie Collins and Eugène Sue, and such works as Henri Becque's *La Parisienne*, from which he maintained that he "learned a lot . . . , not only in technique, but in the matter of fundamental attitude toward life" (*Journal*, December 2, 1903).

When Bennett came to the actual composition he liked to feel that he was putting into practice his theories on mental efficiency. While writing *The Old Wives' Tale*, he bought an "album of modes, 1830–1870" (*Journal*, June 3, 1908); and in sending to Walpole a book chronicling historical facts, he remarked that he had used a copy for some twelve years and that it was the "basis" of *The Old Wives' Tale, Clayhanger*, and similar novels.[21]

Atkins reported that Bennett was completely systematic in working out his plots: "He would divide his scheme into parts which he numbered, and divide each part into sections. He knew in advance what he would put into each

[20] *Journal 1929*, September 25.
[21] May 29, 1913, *Letters*, II, 331.

part and each section." [22] Bennett's own remarks show that such an outline was only loose and tentative. While writing *The Old Wives' Tale*, for example, he worked from scene to scene, sometimes mapping out the action during walks in the forest of Fontainebleau. [23] The comments on the composition of *The Imperial Palace* also suggest a flexible outline. In his *Journal 1929*, he recorded having begun the actual writing September 25 at 3:30 P.M. He continued, "I know the main plot, but by no means all the incidents thereof, though I have a few titbits of episodes which I shall not omit." The use of the gloves from the Goncourts was one of these. The note goes on to say that Bennett had "the whole of the material for the novel; and it is indexed, in a notebook." [24]

There is one small bit of evidence that Bennett sometimes not only did not know "all the incidents" in a story, but was uncertain about key matters as well. In the very slight story "Tiddy-fol-lol" (in *Tales of the Five Towns*, 1905) a man strikes the deaf son of his estranged daughter and the blow on the ear restores the lad's hearing and corrects his stammer. The grandfather's repentance and reconciliation with his daughter naturally follow. A brief jotting in a notebook implies that Bennett had initially achieved an entire plot of some sort before he arrived at the essential element of the final version. He starts with the admonition "Alter the ending," and proceeds, "Make boy a little daft, deaf or something and let the blow cure him." [25] One cannot even guess what kind of ending the

[22] Atkins, *Incidents and Reflections*, p. 177.

[23] *Journal*, October 1 and November 4, 1907.

[24] For brief discussions of the notebooks for novels cf. J. G. Hepburn, "Manuscript Notes for *Lord Raingo*," *English Fiction in Transition*, V, No. 1 (1962), 1–5; "The Notebook for *Riceyman Steps*," *PMLA*, LXXVIII, No. 3 (1963), 257–261; and *The Art of Arnold Bennett*.

[25] In a notebook at Keele University entitled "The Five Towns." The story first appeared in *Lloyd's Weekly Newspaper*, December 30, 1900.

story could have had without the deafness. The motif
was not at all new. In fact, in *A Man from the North* Larch
plans to write a tale with the same title which will concern
a half-witted boy who will be killed by his enraged grandfather. Larch's starkly tragic story would have been
reminiscent of Maupassant. Bennett's own final version is
genial and mildly sentimental.

Certainly the novels, too, underwent extensive revision
of direction and invention of new elements as, keeping
his main direction in mind, Bennett worked from day to
day. It was, after all, not the intricacy of plot that made
the better novels significant, but the substance and tone
of the separate scenes.

When Bennett began to write fiction he had but imper-
fectly mastered the principles he set down for himself, and
a remarkable unevenness was the result. His worst passages are labored, even sentimental. Among them the
following from near the beginning of *Anna of the Five Towns*
are typical: "interchanging thus [by smiles] messages too
subtle and delicate for the coarse medium of words," and,
on the same page, "The crude, brazen sounds were tem-
pered in their passage through the warm, still air, and fell
gently on the ear in soft waves, quickening every heart to
unaccustomed emotions" (12). Fortunately, when two
pages later Bennett began to describe the visual impression
of the Five Towns, he was in his proper element again.

Apart from minor variations he later tried very few
departures from the manner that came natural to him.
One was *The Book of Carlotta* (1905), which some readers
have damned perhaps as much for its style as for its subject
matter, finding both sentimental.[26] In *Carlotta* Bennett let

---

[26] Georges Lafourcade calls the "semi-hysterical" style "simply the
perfection of vulgarity, insincerity and cheap pathos," and he finds the
descriptions "directly reminiscent of Ouida" (*Arnold Bennett: A Study*
[London: Frederick Miller, 1939], p. 91).

his heroine tell her own story of her love for a musical
genius, of the man's degradation as a drunkard, and of his
resurrection under her nursing and inspiration. He quoted
Maupassant in the epigraph, but revealed none of his
restraint in the telling. Instead, Carlotta's own words are
an almost uniform paean so packed with assertions of
emotion that hyperboles soon become the expected and
the emotion itself becomes tame. Any of dozens of passages
will illustrate, if one keeps in mind that they are surrounded
by more of the same. Thus, when Carlotta renounces
Ispenlove, a minor character, she sings out, "Oh, the
cruel joy of that moment! Who will dare to say that the
spirit cannot burn with pleasure while drowning in grief?
Or that tragedy may not be the highest bliss? That instant
of renunciation was our true marriage" (172). Later
Bennett tried to defend the enraptured tone of the book
as a realistic expression of his artistically inclined heroine,
but the simple fact was that the tone was sentimental and
high-flown.

Bennett again tried an impassioned tone in *The Glimpse*,
especially in the rhapsodic account of his hero's vision.
The result is less unsatisfactory mainly because the tempo
of the novel does have some variety and because there is
freshness in the images of the vision. In two plays, *Judith*
(1919) and *Don Juan de Marana* (1923) his purpose was to
create a poetic tone. With all his merits, however, Bennett
was not a poet, least of all a Shelley, and the sought-for
magic is never evoked. What all four works reveal is that
the fine feeling for the romantic which Bennett possessed
could not flourish in a world removed from the realities of
the one he personally knew, that it could not be nourished
by rhetoric foreign to his temperament.

Though in his later serious fiction Bennett rarely slipped
into the sentimental and colorless phrasing we have cited
from *Anna*, like all writers, he found composition a con-

stant struggle to reveal rather than assert. The meaning and emotion in a scene must always be paramount, but the danger was in insistence upon them. Bennett was aware of his shortcomings. Upon rereading *Le Crime et le Châtiment*—by which title we may suppose that he was using a French translation—he praised two scenes as "absolutely full of the most perfect detail." He went on to say, "It really disgusted and depressed me about my own work, which seemed artificial and forced by the side of it. I expect that in most of my work there is too much forcing of the effect, an inability to do a thing and leave it alone" (*Journal*, June 11, 1910).

Granted that even in the serious novels there are artificial touches and that there are passages which are labored and flat, indeed that Bennett came to repeat his own clichés, still what remains in the reader's mind is a sense of honest craftsmanship in the service of a responsive sensibility. To illustrate, we may pluck short excerpts from the first chapters of *The Old Wives' Tale* and *Clayhanger*.

The first five or six pages of the story of Constance and Sophia Baines do what Mrs. Woolf so much deplored, and they do it well. We have the general scene and the house at the bottom of the square. Next we have the two girls looking out the window. We know by now that their own world is a very small place and they must be yearning for any excitement whatever. Suddenly Sophia bursts out with "There she goes!" and through the window we are introduced to the back of the Baines drudge, Maggie, on her one-afternoon-a-month holiday. We shall learn before the end of the paragraph that in seventeen years she has been engaged eleven times. We shall also learn that Sophia tries to feel scorn for her because she is not wearing gloves and that Constance will reply, "Well, you can't expect her to have gloves." All such remarks will tell us much about the two heroines, so that Maggie's setting forth is highly pertinent to the direction of the story. But it is also interesting for itself:

> Up the Square, from the corner of King Street, passed a woman in a new bonnet with pink strings, and a new blue dress that sloped at the shoulders and grew to a vast circumference at the hem. Through the silent sunlit solitude of the Square (for it was Thursday afternoon, and all the shops shut except the confectioner's and one chemist's) this bonnet and this dress floated northwards in search of romance, under the relentless eyes of Constance and Sophia. Within them, somewhere, was the soul of Maggie, domestic servant at Baines's. Maggie had been at the shop since before the creation of Constance and Sophia. She lived seventeen hours of each day in an underground kitchen and larder, and the other seven in an attic, never going out except to chapel on Sunday evenings, and once a month on Thursday afternoons. (*The Old Wives' Tale*, 9)

The artistic method is traditional enough—the presentation of the immediate image, a bit of narration, and a reflective implication. Perhaps the tone, too, may seem usual. And yet the sketch is peculiarly the work of Arnold Bennett, who, having steeped himself in the realists, remained very much a romantic at heart. As we read we not only see Maggie; we may sharpen our perception for seeing. For, simple and unassuming as the sentences are, they are the product of years of observation, reading, and reflection.

In *Clayhanger*, Edwin is walking homeward with his friend Charlie Orgreave after his last day at school. We have been given a general characterization of the Five Towns, where Edwin's life is to unfold, and a glimpse of the lad himself. Bennett now proceeds to paint for us somewhat more precisely the immediate scene:

On their left were two pitheads whose double wheels revolved rapidly in smooth silence, and the puffing engine-house and all the trucks and gear of a large ironstone mine. On their right was the astonishing farm, with barns and ricks and cornfields complete, seemingly quite unaware of its forlorn oddness in that foul arena of manufacture. In front, on a little hill in the vast valley, was spread out the Indian-red architecture of Bursley— tall chimneys and rounded ovens, schools, the new scarlet market, the grey tower of the old church, the high spire of the evangelical church, the low spire of the church of genuflexions, and the crimson chapels, and rows of little red houses with amber chimney-pots, and the gold angel of the blackened Town Hall topping the whole. The sedate reddish browns and reds of the composition, all netted in flowing scarves of smoke, harmonized exquisitely with the chill blues of the chequered sky. Beauty was achieved, and none saw it. (8–9)

To be sure, the "harmonized exquisitely" is bad art, and the editorial comment of the last sentence should have been implicit, not asserted. Both represent a "forcing of the effect." But the rest, a graphic impression enlivened with specific details, sets not only the scene, but the tone for the life of Edwin Clayhanger. There are hints of the Goncourts and of the impressionistic painters; by applying their methods one could give the panorama of any scene. There is also, however, a very personal feeling about Burslem. Bennett does not sentimentally gloss over the ugly; it is all there. But so, too, is the almost miraculous fact that any kind of farm should survive; and atop everything is the gold angel, if not defiant, then at least tolerant of the dirt and smoke all about.

The description is the work of a man who grew up in Burslem, attended and hated its Sunday schools, coughed from its smoke, and marveled at its instinct for life. It is the achievement of an artist who, having lived in London and Paris, returned in imagination to Burslem to seek in its unpromising purlieus the meaning of existence. It is, in short, both naïve and sophisticated; and, without the help—or hindrance—of the final sentence, it brings into a realistic scene the spirit of romance.

CHAPTER FIVE

Pursuit of Spirits
Light and Fair

BENNETT'S CONTEMPORARY, Joseph Conrad, once wrote that a novelist must create a world in which he could "honestly believe." In his most serious works Bennett set himself that task. In many another he abandoned all pretense of normal probability and created a story of suspense and ingenuity over which presided the genial spirit of romance. Sometimes, too, as in *Lord Raingo* and *The Imperial Palace*, on one page he stayed close to reality as we know it and on the next indulged unabashedly in the grandiose and fabulous. Even in such sober novels as *Anna, The Old Wives' Tale, Clayhanger,* and *Riceyman Steps,* "cards" or other eccentrics wander about and prosaic incidents are given a romantic wistfulness.

Though Bennett disparaged his fantasias and spoke but casually of his humorous stories, the fact is that he enjoyed writing them, and he particularly liked to put on the mask of the card. Determined to keep his daily schedule orderly and consistent, he nevertheless enjoyed his rare lapses into some impulsive breach of his self-regimentation. In his fictional cards he merely compounded the impulsiveness.

The charm of a true card resides in the fact that his antics are a surprise most of all to himself. His world is always miraculous, for he can suddenly cast aside all dull common sense and have his own version of an Arabian Night. Psychologically he is hardly aware of what he is doing; rather, he is later astonished at what he has done.

The fantasias and the lighter short stories—and most of the short stories are light—are ingenious farces, and their heroes have only the one or two essential characteristics that will bring about the plot. In "The Burglary" (in *The Grim Smile of the Five Towns*), for example, Sir Jehoshaphat is overscrupulous. Possessing a distasteful portrait which he feels it would be improper to destroy, he can only connive to have it stolen. Unfortunately, the burglar, being a practical man, takes only the expensive frame, along with the household silver. In the fantasias the heroes are likely to be eccentric millionaires. Thus, in *The Grand Babylon Hotel* (1902), when a hotel waiter refuses to serve his daughter bass beer, Racksole finds himself obliged to buy the hotel. Of course, there is villainy afoot in the Grand Babylon, and Racksole and his daughter get a chance to become detectives. In *Hugo* (1906) the variation involves the manager of a gigantic store who is equally given to extravagant exploits. And so on through a number of novels dominated by urbane men and vivacious, self-assured girls who anticipate the detective-story heroines of cinema and television. In *The Vanguard* (1927), Bennett was still mining his vein, now making use of his experiences in yachting to give a freshness to his scene. Even in *The Imperial Palace*, his last major work, there are incidents that might easily adorn a fantasia.

The hero of a fantasia, in short, is really a card. He merely happens to be performing his impulsive acts in a never-never world which has, to be sure, a coherence and logic of its own, but was created deliberately to be unlike anything actual. When we turn to the light works which Bennett did not label fantasias, we do not necessarily come back to reality, though we may; but we are at least close to everyday things. Of course, because the hero is a card, these diurnal affairs become topsy-turvy.

In *Leonora*, which has light touches, old Meschach is a crusty card, who joins his sister in making a game out of willing their property. If she outlives him, the money will eventually go to John Stanway; if Meschach survives, to Fred Ryley. Thus the two will have equal chances, winner take all. In the thin novel *A Great Man* (1904), the main subject is the extravagant antics of Tom Knight. Much better is the short story "His Worship the Goosedriver" (in *Tales of the Five Towns*), in which to defend the honor of Bursley by insisting that it, no less than its great rival, Hanbridge, can support trade, the deputy mayor offers to buy fourteen geese from a gooseherd and, finding his offer accepted, is confronted with driving them home in rain and darkness. Having trapped himself, he at once anticipates a serendipity: "It would be an immense, an unparalleled farce; a wonder, a topic for years, the crown of his reputation as a card" (14). In the denouement his embarrassed wife plays a trick upon him which transforms his undignified prank into a deed of philanthropy. Her triumph typifies the victories of wives over husbands in Bennett: but what one remembers is the comic and generally unsuccessful effort of her husband morally to dominate fourteen recalcitrant geese.[1]

In *The Old Wives' Tale* (1908) young Gerald Scales is at first rather like a card, and Cyril Povey, son of Samuel and Constance, has some of the features. But it is Samuel himself who has the essentials. He is not brilliant, and he is

[1] The Hanley *Evening Sentinel*, March 28, 1931, identifies the hero as Mr. John Aynsley, not of Burslem, but of Longton.

not ingenious, but he can do reckless things. Having acquired a dog, he next proceeds to let Constance know that he intends to have an after-dinner cigar. Bennett comments, "Thus Mr. Povey came out in his true colours as a blood, a blade, and a gay spark" (158). From such triumphs Samuel goes on to violate the sacred Baines tradition against advertising. Ultimately this most unheroic man finds himself immersed in a futile, but noble attempt to save his cousin's life. He is no Racksole nonchalantly buying the Grand Babylon, and much of his life is humdrum; but his impulses are toward adventure and they finally lead him to the most gallant form. Far livelier is young Dick Povey, who begins by riding a "boneshaker" daringly down the square and later turns to fast cars and balloons. Even in the midst of tragedy, as when Maria Critchlow commits suicide, Dick senses romance:

> "Strange, isn't it?" he exclaimed afterwards, "how I manage to come in for things? Sheer chance that I was here to-day! But it's always like that! Somehow something extraordinary is always happening where I am." And this too ministered to his satisfaction and to his zest for life. (594)

The very substance of *Buried Alive* (1908) stems from a cardlike act by the shy artist Priam Farll. On impulse Farll pretends that it is he who has died, not his valet, and he then assumes the identity of the dead man. The treatment he receives permits satire on snobbery and humbug, but Bennett always keeps foremost the fact that Farll is having a lark. He sets the tone early by suggesting that at fifty Farll is particularly ripe for adventure:

> This man had reached the interesting age . . . when you think you understand life, and when you are often occu-

pied in speculating upon the delicious surprises which existence may hold for you, the age, in sum, that is the most romantic and tender of all ages—for a male. . . . A thrilling age. (11)

Then, in 1911, Bennett published the improbable adventures of Edward Henry Machin, born the same day as Bennett himself, May 27, 1867, in Bursley.[2] His mother combined "Edward" and "Henry" to get "Denry," and Bennett added the epithet "the Audacious," all of which he summed up in the simple title *The Card*. Denry begins with escapades which would seem downright wicked were they not instead mischievously clever. He changes his geography score by inserting a "2" before the "7," he fraudulently secures an invitation to a ball, and he becomes a prowler in the magnificent home of the Countess of Chell. He is not at all chivalric in arranging a breakdown of the countess's coach so that he can gallantly rescue her. And he even engages in rather sharp financial practices that impose upon the gullibility of the poor. As for his virtues, for a short while he seduces his mother away from the wretched house which she obstinately refuses to leave, though she finally defeats him to return to her familiar hovel. On impulse he marries sweet, impoverished Nellie instead of the sophisticated, rich widow he has for a second time found alluring; and he saves the reputation of Bursley by buying back a locally reared football hero to regenerate the team. His first real success is in charming the countess, his last, in becoming mayor of Bursley. Denry is ordinarily too busy with ingenious schemes to stop to reflect, but when he makes his first step upward, to membership in the Sports Club, Bennett measures his progress by his sensations: "Denry blushed, quite probably for the last time in his life. And he saw with fresh clearness how great

[2] Bennett later identified the original of *The Card* as H. K. Hales.

he was, and how large he must loom in the life of the town. He perceived that he had been too modest."[3] At the sea-side resort Llandudno, after putting on a series of rocket fêtes, he is able to sum up his success, "By Jove . . . I've wakened this town up!" (113). And when, at the conclu-sion of his recorded adventures, someone asks what Denry has done, "What great cause is he identified with?" he receives the reply "He's identified . . . with the great cause of cheering us all up" (280).

An older, sometimes depressed Denry returns in *The Regent*, in 1913. His sadness comes upon him when he realizes that he is growing old, and he even asks whether life is "worth living." But as soon as he becomes absorbed in an adventure, such as the building of the Regent thea-ter, all weariness evaporates and he is a romantic adven-turer once again. Mr. Prohack, in the novel so entitled (1922), bears some resemblance to the later Machin. Hav-ing no present occupation, he uses his ingenuity for sheer diversion. Finally, in *The Imperial Palace* we have Evelyn Orcham, a hard-working, usually serious, middle-aged hotel manager who makes of his manifold responsibilities a grandiose, indeed fantasia-like existence. The hotel is an empire and he is the harassed emperor. His sober melancholy reflections concern us elsewhere, but it is the spirit of fun that prevails when, for example, he is ad-judicating between a rajah with his retinue and the more imperious wife of an American millionaire. What charac-terizes all these men is their wistful sense of awe whenever they reflect upon what they have done or on the marvels among which they thrive.

That every man is his own hero is a truism in Bennett. In that very fact is the origin of romance. His Five-Towns characters may be wrongheaded or obstinately perverse,

[3] *The Card: A Story of Adventure in the Five Towns* (London: Methuen and Co., 1964), p. 44.

but they have self-respect, and there is something winsome and charming in their efforts to justify their self-love. Indeed, they become transformed into actors or even creators of fiction as they play their idealized roles. Anna Tellwright, for example, feels a "fundamental superiority" to other girls, and by determination she achieves a double role of meek obedience to a tyrannical father and a ladylike graciousness to the world.

In *Whom God Hath Joined* Annunciata feels a British superiority to the French governess Renée. In her condemnation is implied the rigorous Methodistic virtue which is almost the sole basis of her self-respect: "The French were not serious; they were not moral; they were frivolous. *You could not rely on them.* Their women were dolls; their men were wicked, besides being paltry and grotesque to the eye" (115). Annunciata is narrow and rather hard, but there is a brilliant intensity in her pride that can become almost ecstatic. And it is her pride that, without her sensing the fact, turns Sophia Baines's life into a romantic adventure. To be sure, she pays dearly, but without having the instinct to pay she would have been a nonentity.

Many of the light stories have pride or obstinacy at their center. In "The Dog" (in *Tales of the Five Towns*), for example, Ellis Carter's highly respectable family are humiliated because Ellis has been seen with a strolling Wakes girl, but their concern for appearances is overmatched by that of the girl's father. "The Heroism of Thomas Chadwick" (in *The Matador of the Five Towns*) is among the tales that mingle comedy and pathos to arrive at a wistful portrait. Although he has been unable to hold any job for long, Thomas has retained his dignity. Now a tram conductor, he finds a purse belonging to the stingy Mrs. Clayton Vernon and is rewarded with sixpence. When twitted, he lies that she gave him two sovereigns, and even when exposed he sustains his poise. The story concludes with the remark that such a man was unfit to be a tram conductor, "so that he was again thrown upon the world."

In *The Regent* Bennett suggests that people in the Five Towns have fires not for warmth, but for light, and he quips, "Seemingly they use their pride to keep them warm" (15). In *These Twain*, as we have noticed, the inhabitants of Trafalgar Road say to themselves morning and evening as they leave or return to their homes, "Most folks are nobodies, but I am somebody." Indeed, the search for identity in Bennett's stories is commonly an attempt to be somebody. Lady Southminster, for example, in *The Lion's Share*, finding no distinction in her newly acquired lady-ship, returns to the shop where she once worked and sits in the window, ostensibly to advertise a hair restorer, but really to display her beautiful hair.

In the fantasias and most of the serious novels romance is a perquisite of youth. For the shop girls in *Leonora* anticipation of a dance is the very essence of romance— "this bright fallacy, this fleeting chimera, this delusive ecstasy, this shadow and counterfeit of bliss which the goddess [Aphrodite] vouchsafed to her communicants" (212). The dance may be an illusion, but without it reality would be less fine. Youth can, of course, be arrogant and cruel, as Millicent, in the same novel, reveals; but even though Millicent is thoughtlessly selfish, her youthful enthusiasm converts dross into an illusion of beauty. In *The Old Wives' Tale* the opening scenes are once again permeated with the spirit of youthful illusion. Sophia pos-sesses the "confident and fierce joy of youth. . . . 'What on earth equals me?' she seemed to demand with enchanting and yet ruthless arrogance" (15). It will require stunning blows to thwart Sophia's quest for romance.

The determination of girls to defy the irrevocable encroachment of age was indeed a major subject for

Bennett. The certainty of ultimate defeat lent a poignant beauty to their attempts. That they were egoistic became an irrelevance; it was as if, struggling against a cruel fate, they were more courageous then selfish. Of young Audrey, in *The Lion's Share*, Bennett writes:

> She had done nothing herself, she had neither earned money nor created any of the objects which adorned her; nor was she capable of doing the one or the other. Yet she felt proud as well as happy, because she was young and superbly healthy, and not unattractive (121).

What Audrey wants from life is the lion's share, and she can have it only by asserting her youthful feminine charm. When she stops to reflect, she feels that she is a "sham in the world of shams" (344). She cannot afford reflection.

Part of the wonder which Bennett found associated with youth was in its resilience. In *The Price of Love* Rachel suffers cruel disillusionment in her marriage to the weak-willed Louis, whom she comes finally to pity, and yet her tribulations have become for her an adventure in which she can be pleased with her role. At a time when she is in an embarrassing plight she must pretend to her fellow townsmen in the shopping thoroughfare that she is a proud matron confidently walking among them. Bennett describes her sudden transition: "Her heart lay like a weight in her corsage for an instant, and the next instant she was in the bright system again, because she was so young" (260). What makes Hilda Lessways interesting is, once again, a youthful capacity for recovering enthusiasm and, even in middle age, a determination to remain young. It may be added that it makes her pathetic as well.

As one reads the novels he quickly discovers that, like Bennett himself, many of the characters are concerned with the "savour of life." They act, of course, but it is their sensation of their daily existence that matters. They are not sentimentalists, nor are they deliberate hedonists. But even the most prosaic see themselves as the central figures in a world which is never without the possibility of romance.

That romance was really "in the eye of the beholder" was a truism when Bennett first stated the fact in *Journalism for Women*, in 1898, but it was never trite. For the glamor and beauty which the eye unaffectedly and honestly created could but reflect an inner spirit, of whose nature there could be infinite variety. Thus, nursing is a romance of creative adventure for the nurse in *A Man from the North*, who, along with doctors and soldiers, tastes the "true savour of life" (145). In a moment of idyllic freedom Anna Tellwright contemplates her life in the home of her miserly father, and she suddenly realizes that "the monotony, the austerity, the melancholy of her existence had been sweet and beautiful" (192). For Leonora life with a weak, dishonest husband is melancholy, and yet it has been an engrossing adventure in which she has been a gracious, attractive heroine. As Bennett states her thoughts she seems to be saying to an imaginary admirer, "You see that I too have lived through crises, and that I can appreciate how wonderful they are" (251). Not unaware that the most romantic events of her life are probably past and with no exciting prospects ahead, Leonora can still find pleasure in thinking of the decorum with which she has managed her life, of "the calm and the orderliness and the high decency of everything" (327).

Responsibility for shaping the destiny of another was romantic to the point of exaltation. In *Carlotta* the heroine rejoices in the challenge of rescuing her musician lover from drunken degradation. In *The Old Wives' Tale*, when she thinks she can convert Mme. Foucault from being a kept woman, Sophia is happy: "She had a purpose in existence" (404). Rachel, in *The Price of Love*, has the most exacting of responsibilities, having married a thief. In the title itself Bennett implied that there must be a price, and it was as high as he could make it. Yet it was not too high, for without Louis for a husband Rachel would have an uneventful life. With him, she has both a cause for pride and, even more precious, a perilous adventure:

> He was not a clodhopper. . . . He did not drink; he was not a beast. He was not mean. He might scatter money, but he was not mean. In fact, except that one sinister streak in his nature, she could detect no fault. There was danger in that streak. . . . [sic] Well there was danger in every man. She would accept it; she would watch it. Had she not long since reconciled herself to the prospect of everlasting vigil? (320).

In the very vigil itself is the savor, without which all might be blandly insipid.

Perhaps it is also a truism that sadness is beautiful. Again, however, Bennett did much more than merely enunciate his belief or give it sentimental embodiment. In the *Clayhanger* series, for example, he shows repeatedly how Edwin and especially Hilda wring from melancholy circumstance a fleeting revelation of beauty. Most often it accompanies their sense of wonder when they find they can accept the grayness and gloom. Summing up one of Hilda's tribulations, Bennett writes: "She savoured her unhappiness. She drank it down passionately, as though it were the very water of life—which it was" (*Hilda Lessways*, 66). And, not asking much from life, Clayhanger gets unexpected glimpses that allow him to be "at once happy and impregnated with a sense of the frightful sadness that lurks in the hollows of the world" (*These Twain*, 336). Perhaps the best statement of Bennett's feeling that life was essentially romantic is his record of Edwin's sensations at the burial of Auntie Hamps:

And even in that hilly and bleak burial-ground, with melancholy sepulchral parties and white wind-blown surplices dotted about the sodden slopes, and the stiff antipathetic multitude around the pit which held Auntie Hamps, and the terrible seared, harsh, grey-and-brown industrial landscape of the great smoking amphitheatre below, Edwin felt happy in the sensation of being alive and of having to contend with circumstance. (453)

Bennett was intrigued with the fact that the First World War was at once horrible and romantic. George Cannon in *The Roll Call* (1918) finds the army a new world of adventure in which he very quickly experiences an exhilarating fatigue. In *The Pretty Lady* (1918) the war gives G. J. Hoape a new insight into the nature of man:

Morally he was profiting by the war. Nay, more, in a deep sense enjoying it. The immensity of it, the terror of it, the idiocy of it, the splendour of it, its unique grandeur as an illustration of human nature, thrilled the spectator in him.[4]

It is, again, the war that permits Lord Raingo an Indian summer of excitement before he dies.

When writing about Edwin Clayhanger or Hoape, Bennett could draw upon his own sensations as he looked back over his life or as he lived through the war. There was a perspective, however, very different from theirs for which he had to rely heavily upon his imagination. To employ it he created Elsie, the servant girl, who grows up in squalor, works devotedly for the miser Earlforward, falls in love with a shell-shocked, not overly bright young man, and finally achieves the highest success she can dream of in sharing with him a subterranean cell in the house of Dr. Raste, where they work as servants. For Elsie a bedroom all to herself at the Earlforwards' is a wonderful

---

[4] *The Pretty Lady* (London: Cassell, n.d.), p. 195.

luxury, cold, bare, and ugly though it is; and eating whatever comes to hand is a solace in times of stress. In her
inarticulate, bewildered fashion she can feel "both happy
and unhappy." What she knows for sure is that in life
"there were surprises which you expected and surprises
you couldn't be expected to expect."[5] When the little girl
she has cared for is sent off to boarding school and Elsie
returns alone from Victoria Station, she at first feels lost,
and then her grief gives way to hunger. She still has Joe,
to whom she is both wife and mother. The story of Elsie
is certainly an idyll far removed from the life of Arnold
Bennett. Nevertheless, he believed in its essential truth;
Elsie possesses an instinct for savoring whatever experience
unexpectedly comes her way.

As the *Journal* attests, Bennett possessed a Dickensian
interest in the unexpected surprises in human conduct.
Sometimes the fascination was in the fact that conflicting
impulses could exist peacefully in the human breast, each
taking its turn at domination as circumstances permitted.
Thus the moment their mistress has left the house his
fictional servant maids can abandon their decorum,
become boisterous, and even go swinging in the garden;
and the apparently unemotional drudge Maggie can be
betrothed some eleven times. Or the obsequious waiters in
a hotel can discard their masks and become dashing young
blades the moment they are in the open night air.

The most striking examples mingle romance and pathos.
In *The Old Wives' Tale* Samuel Povey and his neighbors
know only that Daniel is a "good fellow"; they have no
notion of his squalid existence with a drunken slattern.
It is when Samuel sees the murdered wife lying on the
sofa that the truth hits him, for there in the room stands
her murderer, Daniel, "neat, spotless, almost stately, the
man who for thirty years had marshalled all his immense

[5] *Elsie and the Child*, p. 35.

pride to suffer this woman, the jolly man who had laughed through thick and thin!" (225).[6]

In *Hilda Lessways* the bigamist Cannon is a mixture of honesty and charlatanism. He deceives Hilda, engages in dishonest business practices, and lets his elderly wife, whom he hates, extricate him from prison. But, having borrowed money from Clayhanger to flee to America, he will repay every penny. Knowing his lack of integrity, the young Hilda nevertheless finds in his suave, self-assured manner a hint of glamor which her dull life has lacked; and later, when he has wasted her inheritance and gone to prison, she still is drawn toward him. Of the two she prefers Edwin Clayhanger, but Cannon has given her glimpses of a romantic mystery. He is a bewildered, lonely person in a hostile universe; yet he asks for no pity, and his pride is the equal of Hilda's own.

One of the most delightful of Bennett's minor characters is Clayhanger's Auntie Hamps. As we have noticed, she is a smirking hypocrite who, though she once sides with Edwin against his father, annoys him with her mawkish, sentimental pretense of piety and her exaggerated propriety, and, even when dying, orders her ill-fed, underpaid maid dismissed because she is pregnant. Beside her deathbed Edwin is astonished at the wretched penury of her private life, an utter contrast to the appearance of ease and refinement which she has tried to present to the world. Then he suddenly realizes that, mean, vindictive, and narrow though she is, she is also wonderful. She has made an exacting lifelong career of acting a role, and despite the reality amid which she has lived almost all the hours of every day, she has never admitted defeat. Edwin's thoughts upon her serve as a choral comment: "The sublime obstinacy of the woman had transformed hypoc-

---

[6] Bennett made use of the murder of his alcoholic wife by a local publican. Cf. Dudley Barker, *Writer by Trade*, p. 84.

risy into a virtue, and not the imminence of the infinite unknown had sufficed to make her apostate to the steadfast principles of her mortal career" (*These Twain*, 444).

In *Riceyman Steps* (1923), Bennett created a hero as remote from himself as was Elsie; for Bennett, unlike Henry Earlforward, was no miser. He had always been intrigued, however, by miserliness. Tellwright and other Five-Towns characters get much more pleasure out of saving money than out of producing income, and in his *Journal* Bennett accumulated anecdotes of miserliness. In *Riceyman Steps* he made the habit so romantically enticing that it ceases to be a vice and becomes almost a virtue— simply because the saving of money gives purpose to Earlforward's life and brings out such creativity as he possesses. It even unites husband and wife, for though inclined to be expansive upon festive occasions, Violet at first reservedly and then with devotion adopts her husband's ways. The wedding over, Henry asks her for the pound he has given her the day before; and Bennett comments: "This was the end of the honeymoon; or, if you prefer it, their life was one long honeymoon."[7] Violet must take second place to Henry's high ambition—"his grand passion and vice" (151); but she can acquiesce because even for her "this lovely cash satisfied the soul" (164). There is, of course, once again the pathetic side of the medal, as the two die of starvation and lack of medical care. It might be argued, too, that they could better have helped mankind by some noble work. And yet, they have harmed no one, and even Elsie has loved her existence as their virtual slave. Moral issues being thus irrelevant, the fascination about Henry and Violet is, as with Auntie Hamps, their exalted steadfastness to their ideal, the precious source of their affinity.

Indeed, in both the pocket philosophies and the fiction

[7] *Riceyman Steps* (London: Cassell, n.d.), p. 119.

Bennett reiterates the romance of commonplace life. At times, especially in the early novels, he may protest too much when he should instead be occupied with representation, but even then he escapes from sentimental softness because he refuses to gloss over the ugliness and pain. The things he admires have managed to survive in spite of circumstances that are neither good nor beautiful; and if the adventures are ordinary enough, the sense of wonder with which his characters view them is justified. As we recognized at the outset, Bennett was no philosopher, and he was also neither a Wordsworth nor a Whitman. Nevertheless, he could find excitement in casual daily experience. In *A Man from the North*, for example, Richard Larch perceives a "cloud-like delicacy" in the steam from a railroad engine in smoke-shrouded Bursley, and he senses the "latent poetry of the suburbs" in London. The novel is limited in artistic execution, but its subject matter is challenging. Living a lower middle-class existence and mingling with those who have little of what is labeled culture, Larch has as full a life as his imagination permits, absorbed in his work and his search for love.

The very reason for the unprepossessing appearance of the potteries was, for Bennett, romantic. For the creation of palls of smoke and of ugly scars in the earth merely accompanied the creation of something useful and often beautiful—and not by the brilliant stroke of one mind, but through cumulative accretion, with a multitude of separate labors coordinated for a social purpose. As Anna Tellwright contemplates the finished pottery, it seems to her "a miraculous, almost impossible, result; so definite, precise, and regular after a series of acts apparently variable, inexact, and casual; so inhuman after all that intensely human labour; so vast in comparison with the minuteness of the separate endeavours" (*Anna*, 147).

All commercial activity invited play of the imagination.

In *Leonora*, for example, the train at the station has only paused "in its mighty rush from one distant land of romance to another" (197). In time the complex organization of a great hotel was to be the subject matter for the romance of adventure *The Imperial Palace*. From *The Old Wives' Tale* to *Mr. Prohack* and *Lord Raingo* Bennett was to maintain that it is in his daily work, even if as for Mr. Prohack it consists of manufactured duties, that man most consistently finds his satisfactions. "This is as near a regular happiness as I am ever likely to get" is a summing up that fits not only Bennett himself engaged in his daily stint of writing, but such persons as Constance Baines Povey and Edwin Clayhanger.

A superficial summary of Edwin's career makes it sound ultrabourgeois. From frugal beginnings he rises to moderate affluence, by self-education he acquires some vestiges of culture, he marries an attractive wife, and he is a conscientious employer in a system of employment still rather feudal. The romance of his life, however, is not in its success. It is in the texture of his complex and often frustrating contention with the vexations which await him nearly everywhere. He is never without worry, and he is never unaware of the dirt and smoke of the Five Towns or of "the tedious intimacy of their existence" (*These Twain*, 291). Yet, despite the contrast of the countryside in Devon, where, on a visit, he at first imagines life to be idyllic, he is eager to return home, for only in his work amidst the ugliness can he fulfill himself.

If one gave his fancy a certain rein, he could present the affairs of daily life as they are observed by an impartial and unimaginative participant and the same incidents as they are recast by an artist's imagination. This might, as in "The Death of Simon Fuge," result in high romance. When Loring, the narrator, comes to Bursley, he walks in mud made black with coal dust, and he is surrounded by the "squalid ugliness" of which we have spoken. By detaching himself, however, from the immediate physical discomfort he is able to apprehend the "sublime" vastness worthy of the pen of Dante. His host, Brindley, and Brindley's friend, Colclough, are both combinations of card and genius, who manage their businesses as if incidentally and live for the sake of such things as musical duets on the piano. But of most interest are the two sisters whom the artist Fuge once rowed on a lake at night and the variant accounts of that expedition.

According to the one sister, the pleasant, but unimaginative wife of Colclough, the event had been at best amusing, with Fuge losing an oar and almost upsetting the boat, and she had once dozed off before they returned to shore. In contrast, the story which Fuge has given to the world implies a virtual tryst with two lovely girls, almost an embarkation for Cytherea. When Mrs. Colclough reads his version as narrated in his obituary, she merely remarks, "Yes, from the things Annie used to tell me about him sometimes, I should say that was just how he *would* talk." [8] But what of her forty-year-old sister, Annie Brett, the unmarried barmaid at the Tiger? She has had little to say when told that Fuge is dead, and she has soon turned to banal small talk. But she has almost blushed, and tears have formed during a brief silence. Brindley later remarks that she was once beautiful. The version which Fuge has concocted is the work of an artist interested in things not as they actually were, but as he would have them. Still, his narrative may be much truer than Sally Colclough's in so far as it concerns him and Annie Brett. In writing the story Bennett was not allegorizing. Nevertheless, he was dealing with the fundamental question of the reliability of the artistic imagination. When one created a romantic portrait of life he might very properly believe in its truth.

[8] *Tales of the Five Towns*, p. 307.

Bennett's depiction of the love of men and women lacks the subtlety of James's and the brilliance of Meredith's, and it is never so moving as Hardy's. Rather, it belongs in a tradition that includes Fielding and Jane Austen and much of Scott, Thackeray, and Dickens. Even in the better novels there is much of what might be called wholesome playfulness, sometimes verging on the sentimental, but rescued by humor. Both the pocket philosophies and the novels reiterate the fact that marriage requires adjustment of one's expectations to make for a cooperative adventure. The most recurring assumption is that women like to mother their husbands and that men happily yield to their attentions. Another is that women are ruled by heart and men by reason, though the evidence of the latter is not always convincing. Certainly, in repeatedly making use of such motifs Bennett was not original, and he was but mildly interesting.

Yet in his representation of the essentials of marriage he did achieve a freshness, for here he was able to find the glimpses of romance without which life might be desolate indeed. He started with frank recognition of the egoism of men and women and the fact that any attempt to make a life together meant a clash of wills. In *The Old Wives' Tale*, for example, Samuel Povey sees himself as the "seat of government" and Constance and their son Cyril as "a sort of permanent opposition" (212). In the *Clayhanger* trilogy Hilda uses much the same metaphor to describe Clayhanger on the one hand and herself and her son George on the other.

For many Bennett women a man is a musical instrument on which to test their skill, and Hilda fancies herself a "virtuoso." In fact, deprived of useful activities outside the home, they have little else in which to find self-expression. As for the men, they are inevitably drawn toward women, often of the most diverse kinds. A Samuel

Povey can settle for a pleasing companion with little imagination and not much capacity for bringing surprises into his life. For Larch in *A Man from the North*, for George Cannon in *The Roll Call*, and for a number of others the lure is the strangeness of the culture which they associate with specific women. A few, including Ridware in *Whom God Hath Joined* and Ussher in "The Woman Who Stole Everything," are entrapped by sinister lamias. Others, most notably late in Bennett's career, and most strikingly the industrialist Lucas of *Accident*, are indissolubly attached to virtual furies. Mrs. Lucas, a haggard woman who constantly nags her husband, tells the narrator that married life has been hell, and then she adds, "Well, of course, I like Hell . . . Hell's the great place for romance."[9] In those words she reveals the affinity which, in spite of the wretchedness, has made the marriage enthralling.

The most extended study of the romance of marriage is, of course, the story of Edwin Clayhanger and Hilda Lessways. We know that Helen of Troy was beautiful because Homer insists that she was. Bennett likewise insisted upon the bonds that held Edwin and Hilda as man and wife, no matter how grave the discords. Significantly, Part I of *These Twain* bears the heading "The Woman in the House." It is not a Coventry Patmore angel nor even a Victorian lady that Bennett is talking about, but an impulsive, willful, experienced woman of thirty-five who has borne a son to a bigamist, has endured destitution trying to manage a boarding house, and now has married the man she kissed ten years before.

Hilda is a creature of inconsistencies. She has been able to drudge, and yet she is extravagant. She wants Edwin to be successful, but, like the artist's mistress in Zola's *L'Oeuvre*, she is jealous of his work. She is generous in supporting the cause of the laboring classes, but she thought-

[9] *Accident* (New York: Doubleday, Doran and Co., 1929), p. 49.

lessly tyrannizes over individual employees. She exults in
her independence, but measures her importance by conventional standards. She wishes to be cultivated, but is
almost uncouth in artistic taste. Though she has read
Crashaw, she is not preoccupied with religious or even
poetic reflection. Quite the contrary; for her scornful
glance at the clergyman Peartree seems to say, "What is
all this talk of heaven and hell? I am in love with life and
the senses, and everything is lawful to me, and I am above
you" (*These Twain*, 44).

The mild, outwardly prosaic, and usually predictable
Edwin lacks a "quality heroic, foolish, martyr-like" which
drew Hilda to Cannon. But she imaginatively transforms
him into an oriental tyrant with herself as his queenly
slave. She is proud of his wisdom, but confident in the
superiority of her own. She is not really a sensualist, and
yet there is a fierceness in her kissing of Edwin. She desperately wants a successful marriage, and yet she has no
wish to dissolve her personality to secure it. Bennett
interprets her thoughts: "We are in love. And we love.
I am yours. You are mine. Life is very fine after all. I
am a happy woman. But still—*each is for himself in this
world* and that's the bedrock of marriage as of all other
institutions" (*These Twain*, 136). As the trilogy ends Edwin
can be expected to humor Hilda by buying Ladderidge
Hall. Heart has thus once more triumphed over head. To
call Hilda selfish, however, is to miss the essentials. She
does love Edwin. For her happiness he has been impractical
and chivalric, and she is grateful. In short, far more even
than Cannon, he has made her existence romantic.

As for Edwin, he is very much the plain man, but with
a capacity for wonder, and it is Hilda who first gives him
a sense of mystery. She is only from Turnhill; but when he
first meets her, he becomes aware of another world far
removed from the dull universe in which he has been a

mere underpaid workman in his father's shop. Her kissing him marks the end of the life he has known and hints of a troubled, but exciting future. He is not suddenly freed from oppressive circumstance, but, to borrow Hardy's phrasing, he has changed suddenly from a mere restive creature to a "fettered god." It is his love of Hilda that will sustain him and even help him to break loose, so far as man is capable of doing so, from the circumstantial bonds. By the end of *Clayhanger* Edwin has come to know Hilda for a bewildered, suffering mortal who has not even played fairly with him. But she has recompensed him by drawing him out of himself, and the book ends, "He braced himself to the exquisite burden of life."

When the two are married, Hilda is a new kind of burden. Edwin is democratic, inclined at times toward socialism, and Hilda represents the *ancien régime*. The business, he reflects, "existed with its dirt, noise, crudity, strain, and eternal effort so that she might exist in her elegance, her disturbing femininity, her restricted and deep affections, her irrational capriciousness, and her strange, brusque commonsense" (*These Twain*, 317). Moreover, Edwin is superior to Hilda intellectually. He reads more books, tries to cultivate an appreciation of music, and has better taste in art; and he is something of a philosopher. Yet Hilda is no seductress to dissuade him from noble pursuits. He not only can accept "her impulsiveness, her wrongheadedness, her bizarre ratiocination." They are for Edwin "part of the incomparable romance of existence" (*These Twain*, 421). Edwin is not a dashing, glamorous passionate man. His main virtues are patience and tenacity. Unlike Emily Brontë's Catherine Earnshaw, he could never have said, "I *am* Hilda." On the other hand, it would not occur to him to say that "each is for himself in this world." At no time in the trilogy is there a close communion between husband and wife; each remains strange to the other. But Edwin would not wish to destroy the veil between them. It is the actual, most imperfect woman who, with the help of that veil, has stood as model for his idealization and made it possible for him to sum up his marriage. "What a romance she has made of my life!"

CHAPTER SIX

Invocation of the
Darker Muse

IN SPITE OF THE warm winds and sunshine in Bennett's serious novels, there is somewhat more of the melancholy of gray, chill late afternoons. Summer's lease is temporary and insecure, and the year belongs to the seasons of decay and death. In *The Old Wives' Tale*, the *Clayhanger* series, *Lord Raingo*, and in passages in other novels the reader is aware that the conditions of human life have not been divinely arranged for man's physical or spiritual comfort. Bennett's characters, to be sure, do not, like Hardy's Tess, lament bitterly that they are in a blighted universe, nor is their defeat, if they do succumb, so shattering as that of Jude. Rather, unless struck down by death itself, they persist in their course and usually, in time, become inured. In their inurement is revealed the strength or tolerance of the human spirit, but also the price which it must pay.

Though Bennett felt revulsion against the Calvinistic Methodism of his childhood home, he could only try, as we have noticed, to replace it with Stoicism. Now, Stoicism might be justified intellectually with a totally different sequence of arguments, and its ethical implications might be somewhat different, too. But what mattered, after all, was one's emotional response to existence, and in this the difference between Calvinism, however Methodistic, and Stoicism was by no means distinct. This was, of course, because man begins with his sensations of existence and, whatever his ingenious efforts to fit them into one or another religious or philosophical system, they do not readily change.

It was the Stoicism in Bennett that drew him to the Calvinistic characters of his tales of the Five Towns. The most Calvinistic of these is Ephraim Tellwright, father of Anna of the Five Towns. Ephraim was reared to fear joy as an illusion and to feel secure only when free from its allure. After we have witnessed his tyranny and almost unalloyed miserliness, Bennett lets us see Ephraim's own view of his deeds:

> If you had told him that he inflicted purposeless misery not only on others, but on himself, he would have grinned again, vaguely aware that he had not tried to be happy, and rather despising happiness as a sort of childish gewgaw (*Anna*, 153).

Ephraim does not need any special inspiration to help him endure; sheer pride in his strength is sufficient. Sarah Vodrey, the old servant of Titus Price, typifies the Methodist who found in martyrdom itself a self-glorification that was almost exhilarating. At her death Bennett remarks that she "had never lived save in the fetters of slavery and fanaticism. After fifty years of ceaseless labour, she had gained the affection of one person, and enough money to pay for her own funeral" (280).

Anna Tellwright, like Bennett, finds Methodism distasteful. Her horror springs, however, not so much from its Calvinistic tinge as from the unctuousness of its practitioners. Salvation through subscription to Methodistic dogma would not only be a dreary experience; because of the public exhibition it required of one's innermost feelings, it would be for Anna an embarrassing one. Her self-respect makes her tremble at the thought of stripping one's soul naked at a religious assembly. Nevertheless, though untainted by the mawkish sentimentality of institutional Methodism, Anna is still a child of the Five Towns, and she cannot gainsay her heritage. At the end of the novel, when Willie Price, whom she has loved, has committed suicide and she is to marry a man she respects but does not really love, Bennett writes of her resignation, "She had sucked in with her mother's milk the profound truth that a woman's life is always a renunciation, greater or less" (297).

The picture of Hilda at the close of *Hilda Lessways* is not quite so somber as the parallel one at the end of *Clayhanger*, for the last words express a hope that Hilda will recapture some of the enthusiasm of her youth—a wish to be fulfilled in *These Twain*. But at the moment she is desolate. Earlier she has felt important in being needed by the aged and ill Sarah, her sister-in-law; now she detests her, "and yet by her conscience she was for ever bound to her" (529). Brighton has become for Hilda a "colossal and disgusting enlargement" of her own boardinghouse kitchen. Herself pregnant, when she sees the pregnant unmarried Flossie on the street she blushes "with shame and pity." Then, although not consciously a Calvinist, she assesses her own conduct and bitterly acquiesces in the verdict: "She had sinned. She admitted that she had sinned against some quality in herself. But how innocently and how ignorantly! And what a tremendous punishment for so transient a weakness!" (532). Theologically a distinction can, of course, be made between sinning against a Methodist god and sinning against a quality in oneself, but the sensation of life may still be much the same.

Lord Raingo is concerned with a very different milieu than *Anna* and the *Clayhanger* trilogy. The hero is neither a Calvinist nor a Stoic, but a somewhat comic and bewildered man. So far the story is in the pattern of the light novels, such as *Mr. Prohack*, with an occasional hint of *The Grand Babylon Hotel*. Yet there is in the world of Sam Raingo a tone of weariness and bleakness. His wife dies in an ambiguous automobile accident that may represent suicide, he cannot talk confidentially with his shell-shocked son, and his mistress commits suicide. Finally, he himself contracts pneumonia and dies. These circumstances, of course, strongly color the story, but beyond them there seems to be a loneliness inherent in existence. Sam appears destined for a melancholy end; and at last, despite the dodges he uses to avoid facing the inevitability of death, his spirit is burnt out. Between *Anna* in 1902 and *Lord Raingo* in 1926 Bennett had broken some of his ties with the Five Towns, and he was no longer so much under the shadow of George Moore and the French naturalists. But his sense of the gray oppressiveness of life had merely undergone refinement.

Some kinds of sorrow were inevitable from the nature of mortality, and they could be comprehended, however hard they were to accept, but others left their victims stunned. Such is the blow that hits Myatt in "The Matador of the Five Towns" (1908), when he returns home from being a hero on the football field to experience the loss of his wife in childbirth. Myatt is a rather stolid man, unaware that the owners of the team are exploiting him, ignorant indeed of the injustices that accompany fate. In the moment of his misfortune he is unable to call upon religion or philosophy or poetry to fit his grief into a universal scheme; he is simply baffled.

In the history of Mr. Haim in *The Roll Call* the pathos has a multiple cause. Though a mere factotum, the old man has tried to maintain the illusion of a successful career, and it has given respectability to his age. His latter-day marriage to a charwoman is a mute expression of his faith that, in a subdued way, life can still offer romance. First comes the shock of his daughter's rejection of the marriage, which reduces the self-assured man of dignity to an "almost hysterical" figure of woe. The wife is a pathetic, fragile woman, for whom marriage to an old man and life in a frugal home represent the nearest approach to happiness for which she can hope and pregnancy something especially nice. Her death in childbirth is the denial of even a twilight contentment for a simple and courageous woman. For Haim it is, of course, a drop into the abyss. Bennett sums up the event as seen by George Cannon, significantly ending with a visual detail that adds to the gloom: "It was a terrible house . . . the widower solitary on the ground floor; the dead bodies, the wastage and futility of conception and long bearing up in the bedroom. And in all the house the light of one candle!"[1]

Long before he wrote the story *Accident* Bennett was intrigued with the fact that an unexpected event of hardly a moment's duration could demolish a man's world, render meaningless whatever philosophy he had conconstructed, and destroy the very personality which he had struggled to maintain. "The Hungarian Rhapsody" (in *Tales of the Five Towns*) has a happy and only mildly interesting conclusion. Its most intense scene, however, has a tragic tone. Edward Norris has been injured in a fall from a cab, and Bennett records his assessment of his new identity:

> He was no longer Edward Norris, the finely regulated intelligence, the masterful volition, the conqueror of the world and of a woman; but merely the embodiment of a

[1] *The Roll Call* (London: Hutchinson & Co., 1918), p. 125.

frightened, despairing, flickering, hysterical will-to-live, which glanced in terror at the corners of the room as though it saw fate there. (105)

Drawing upon his own involvement in the railroad accident at Nantes, when, as we have noted, he had let his own affairs lead him to a swift departure from the scene, Bennett revised the incident in his novel *Accident* (1929) and gave to its victim much the same discovery as Norris's. He describes Alan Frith-Walter's sensation as the train crunches to a shattering halt in the night:

> Only a few seconds earlier he had been secure, proud, assessing the far future without any sense of the ridiculousness of so doing. Now the future was brutally, implacably lopped to the limit of another few seconds, and he had been diminished to a helpless insect under the indifferent heel of fate. He felt sick, without manhood, without dignity or self-respect. (169)

Again the narrative goes on to other things, but the recognition remains its most intense scene. There was something incomprehensible in a cosmic order that could unceremoniously deprive a human being of dignity and self-respect.

In a number of Bennett's stories illness is depicted as an affront to man's sensibilities. In *The Glimpse* Loring describes his humiliation when stricken: "I was ashamed of the helpless, brutish condition to which acute pain had abased me. I had an instinctive idea that I owed an apology for it to my fellow-creatures" (119). In *Hilda Lessways* Sarah Gailey, defeated by age and illness, is "degraded and humiliated by mere physical anguish to the condition of a brute" (522). Both Darius Clayhanger and Auntie Hamps die miserably in a dogged decline. In *Riceyman Steps* Joe's illness reveals the nakedness of egoism:

"He wanted, and wanted ravenously, something from everybody he saw. The world existed solely to succour him" (272). That man was inevitably egoistic to a degree did not disturb Bennett. The impulse could find expression in concern for living decently and could elevate the lives of others, but only so long as the conscious will was in control. Without that monitor, man could become a contemptible creature, and even pity could not assuage the horror of his lot.

The cruelty of circumstance as portrayed by the naturalists had been among the subjects which had drawn Bennett to their works. Sometimes in his own writing it is an uncomplicated matter, the victim being merely a defenseless innocent sufferer. Such is Willie Price in *Anna of the Five Towns*, who must endure the humiliation of being the son of a bankrupt thief. Such, too, is Janet Orgreave, who has been given a comfortable home by her parents, but must eventually, because of her fine conscience, be their virtual slave. Already in *Anna* Bennett had stated the issue: "Anna had noticed that in families the youngest, petted in childhood, was often sacrificed in maturity. It was the last maid who must keep her maidenhood, and, vicariously filial, pay out of her own life the debt of all the rest" (222). Willie commits suicide; Janet's life is one of "tragic futility"; her parents "had existed, morally, on Janet for many years, monopolized her, absorbed her, aged her, worn her out, done everything but finish her— and they had made no provision for her survival" (*These Twain*, 206). It was of the Janet Orgreaves that Bennett was thinking when he wrote of the proper education of women. Without the tradition of literal human sacrifice, society was still exacting an immolation almost as cruel.

For girls of servant rank society did not offer even physical comfort in return for slavery. As we have noticed, Hilda, watching young Florrie scrubbing the floor, feels acute shame—"It amounted to barbarism." Florrie does escape—by consoling an unattractive man who makes her pregnant. In *Riceyman Steps* an even more desolate picture is given of an impoverished young woman who has sacrificed beauty and independence to become a childbearing, neurotic wife. With no money, an ailing improvident husband, a hatred of housework, and no hope of surcease from childbearing, she sees herself as "a hag, with five hundred insatiable children everlastingly in tears for something impossible to obtain for them" (49). Although, as we noticed in chapter 2, Bennett protested against the social system that created Janets and Florries and which headed lower-class girls toward a lifetime of poverty, he recognized that the pathos of their lot was perhaps inherent in the nature of things. Through the centuries civilization had been unable to exorcise the cruelty of one person to another. It required more than good intentions to remove the injustices, because the harshness of man to man grew from his sense of the harshness of his own fate and his purblind efforts to assuage it.

Psychologically more interesting are the persons for whom character and circumstance work together to make their lives pitiful. Of these is Mme. Foucault, of *The Old Wives' Tale*, extravagant and sentimental, but also sensitive and affectionate. Sophia Baines Scales considers her a fool because she is not even practical as a kept woman; worse yet, from a Five-Towns view, she is a slattern. But the short history of Mme. Foucault reveals that she is trying, sometimes frantically, to maintain her self-respect, and that defeat is inevitable. She has had only sexual attractiveness and has had to depend on the illusion that men need her. Now that age is winning, she must throw herself degradingly on the mercies of an indifferent man. With her and the later prostitute Christine of *The Pretty Lady* Bennett incidentally attacks the ills of a hypocritical nineteenth-century society. Rather more, however, he seems to be saying that by the very nature of the sexes women are tempted to plunge toward tragedy. Only Sophia and others of her strength can find self-expression and with it self-esteem except as the satellites of men; and even the strong, such as Hilda Lessways, may find themselves in an oriental role. Had Mme. Foucault had the good fortune to marry well, she would have had security, but she would still have lost the beauty, crude though it was, on which depended her identity. Significantly, Sophia does not call her a sinner. Indeed, she does not injure others, and the alternative in life for her and for Christine to survive would have been some brutal form of drudgery, at the expense of renunciation of all they have believed winsome in their femininity.

A special case is Queenie Paulle, in *The Pretty Lady*, who is a war casualty because even the war has not let her reconcile the conflicting urges that impel her. She and her mother have organized support for hospitals in France, but about all she can do is to arrange charity bazaars—a fatuous enterprise. She also dresses expensively, reasoning that it is good for men's morale to see well-dressed women. But her role is futile; she wants to be a woman and she wants to be doing something splendidly heroic. Bazaars are a poor outlet, and in her neurasthenic state she climbs to a rooftop during an air raid to make believe that she "*is* . . . on the Front" (223). Her consequent death is not quite a suicide, and yet it is the end of a spirit for which no bright morning could ever have dawned.

There are two characters whom Bennett may have created as tests of his own compassion, for both are rascals. The one is the hypocritical Sunday-school superintendent, Titus Price, in *Anna of the Five Towns*. Titus is an incompetent business man and a thief. But his harassment by Ephraim Tellwright has been more terrible than man should have to endure. Lacking the grand heroism of a classic protagonist, Titus has had to resort to devious, petty ways to survive and hold up to the world a pretense of personal worth and dignity. Finally even these will not suffice and he commits suicide. That Titus is a scheming, almost contemptible creature who can only seek to evade his fate, not to fight back, makes him singularly pathetic for Bennett. Personally, the novelist would not have liked Titus, nor would he wade into sentimentality to shed tears upon him. But every man has to reckon with a fate which will possibly destroy him, and Titus has been no more an egoist in his concern for self-preservation than most others. The very nature of his existence has been degrading, and it is rather wonderful that he has for so long been able to pretend that it has not.

If a distinction is permissible, the second rascal, the senior George Cannon, is a charlatan rather than a hypocrite. He has deserted his elderly wife, he is unabashedly dishonest in business affairs, and besides irresponsibly losing Hilda's money, he gets her pregnant. Still his imprisonment is a terrible thing. When Hilda and Clayhanger see him marching along a prison corridor, they can only be ashamed for his abject humiliation. Bennett offers little commentary, but the scene is a vivid revelation of the tragic cruelty of man to man. Cannon has been wicked, and the only means that society has been able to invent to deal with wickedness is itself accursed. There is an implied indictment of nineteenth-century prisons. Beyond that, however, is a suggestion that, in his bewilderment about human nature, man can only resort to destruction, making wretched what at best is sad enough.

If marriage could bring romance, it could also create tragedy. Having depicted two wrecked marriages in *Whom God Hath Joined* and others in *The Old Wives' Tale* and

These Twain, Bennett returned to the subject in *Lord Raingo*. Here neither of the partners is a bad person. Sam and Adela have simply been unable to find romance together, and each has contributed to the wasting of the other's life. Now, as Adela lies lifeless on the bed, Sam looks at her "lined, dry features" and remembers his hopes years before, when their son was about to be born. No one thing has destroyed the marriage; it has merely been a failure. Bennett records Sam's reflections: "He had desired such a home [attractive and hospitable] more than anything; but she could not create it for him. She had rendered his wealth futile. Not her fault; nobody's fault" (172). The meditation continues: "Compassion! Sadness! Weariness! And again compassion? On the bed lay the symbol and summing up of all the war-grief and fatigue of the world" (173). To live free from terror in an unknown world man desperately seeks affinity with another soul. Between Adela and Sam even the illusion of affinity has faded long ago, and nowhere, not even with his young, affectionate mistress Delphine will Sam find what marriage has not provided.

One might survive accidents and recover from will-crushing illness, and he might miss most of the vicissitudes that weakness of character and ill luck could bring. But unless he died young, the sensation of age was likely to descend upon him as an ominous shadow. In "Rabbi Ben Ezra" Browning did not really deal with the issue of growing old, for though chronologically advanced, the rabbi has still all his faculties and a youthful spirit. In the aged Constance Baines Povey, Bennett comes nearest to accord with Browning, for in spite of her sciatica, Constance is almost as excited about daily affairs as when she was young, and she does not long ruminate upon the fact that she was once a playful girl and is now a fat old woman. Constance is not, however, typical for Bennett,

whose characters are repeatedly the victims of the relentless deterioration that may come slowly or, again, with a
leap, to leave them stunned with the sense of what they
have lost, or—equally pathetic—to deprive them of the
very memory of what they once possessed and reduce them
to mere suffering creatures under a torture that will not
end till death.

The decline of his father and the last distressing hours
of his mother, as we have noted, remained painfully vivid
for Bennett. The list of persons in his fiction who descend
into helplessness and death would be almost as long as a
list of the serious novels themselves. In *A Man from the North*
Mr. Aked dies struggling for breath. At Uncle Meschach's
disintegration Leonora feels that "every grief, anxiety,
apprehension, was joy itself compared to this supreme
tragedy of natural decay" (*Leonora*, 271). Of Lord Francis,
Carlotta writes, "The fact of my presence had dropped
like a pebble into the strange depths of that aged mind, and
the waters of the ferocious egotism of senility had closed
over it, and it was forgotten" (*Carlotta*, 191). John Baines
is both physically repellent and senile. The young Sophia
wishes to feel sympathetic, but her father is "tragically
ridiculous . . . a ferocious egoist, like most bedridden
invalids, out of touch with life." (*The Old Wives' Tale*, 53).

Darius Clayhanger, once the strong-willed master who
would not give quarter to anyone, becomes a child again
with the softening of his brain. Edwin, who has endured
most from his father, can only say to himself, "What a
damned shame!" to which Bennett adds, "Meaning that
destiny had behaved ignobly to his father, after all.
Destiny had no right to deal with a man so faithlessly"
(*Clayhanger*, 376). Before Darius finally gives up his
hideous existence he becomes a "loathsome object"
imprisoned for weeks on his bed. Of old Mr. Shushions,
formerly a kindly man, but now a senile, foolish one,

Bennett writes, "Mr. Shushions' sole crime against society was that he had forgotten to die" (252). With no relative to care for him, he can only expire at last in a workhouse.

Sam Raingo's last days are a mixture of illusion and stark reality. Struck down by illness, he is "afraid, in a sense in which he had never been afraid before. Nothing and nobody mattered, not even Delphine, save this fear" (*Lord Raingo*, 305). Of a resilient nature, he soon finds some self-importance in the fact that his illness is of public concern. But when he reads of Delphine's suicide, his egoistic refuge is smashed: "He was alone, like a child or a dog that has been lost for hours and given up hope of ever being found again. He was as distressingly and intolerably alone as in his delirium, edging away from the precipice [of death] and the dark river" (316). In his last moments he is still alone, "in the awful void" (393).

What of life when pain and death are not immediately present, when existence merely stretches on into a vista where lights seem, one by one, to go out with the passing of years? Here we have to deal with women in Bennett's novels, sometimes women who are still far from aged, but who apprehend the coming of age. For Bennett one of the truisms of life was that women—at least sensitive women— died twice, the first time when they lost their beauty. In *Our Women* (1920) he was to pronounce dogmatically, "But for a woman there is no full and genuine compensation for the departure of beauty and freshness" (183). Behind his assertion was the assumption that even in the Western world women instinctively inclined toward an oriental role. Though he scolded and cajoled them and demanded that they strive for independence, their fulfilment as human beings was rarely dependent on intellectual pursuits and creative work. It rested, first of all, on personal charm and poise, which might be cultivated, but which were assisted by beauty and youthful spirits.

And Bennett himself would not minimize the value of feminine loveliness. Even independence was no compensation for its loss. And lost it would probably be, so that ravaging age was a specter lurking in the recesses of a looking glass.

As we noticed in chapter 1, the thought of a woman's aging was indeed an obsession with Bennett. Witness a typical note from 1914 in *From the Log of the Velsa*, in which the tone has only deepened since he wrote in his *Journal* ten years before of the two young French girls whose "fleeting charm . . . was so soon to fade." On the quay at Spotsbjerg he had seen a "young and pretty girl leaning on her father's, or grandfather's shoulder." The specter was there, too, unseen perhaps by the girl, but very real for Bennett, as he noted simply, "Full of the thought that she would one day be old and plain, we fled from Spotsbjerg" (136).

In *Leonora* the forty-year old heroine is not for long able to forget that, though still attractive, she is on the brink of change. She envies her daughter Ethel for being young: "Youth! She would have forfeited all her experience, her knowledge, and the charm of her maturity, to recover the irrecoverable!" (10). After a visit from her lover, Arthur, she looks in the mirror and, although she sees that she has not yet lost her loveliness, she nevertheless apprehends the inevitable. At the moment she does not think of her husband's financial trouble, "nor his deviousness, nor even his mere existence." Her only thought is "Oh! That I were young again!" (105).

Before she has seen human degradation Carlotta, of *The Book of Carlotta*, is callous to the suffering of others. In her unconscious cruelty, however, she records truths that cannot be ignored. Of her rival, Mrs. Ispenlove, whose husband has become infatuated with Carlotta, she writes: "Gray hair, wrinkles, crow's feet, tired eyes, drawn mouth,

and the terrible tell-tale under the chin—these were what
I saw in Mary Ispenlove. She had learnt that the only
thing worth having in life is youth. I possessed everything
that she lacked" (141).

When Clayhanger once again meets Hilda, now at
thirty-four the worn manager of a boardinghouse, he
reflects that it is "a poignant shame that time and sorrow
and misfortune could not pass over a young girl's face and
leave no mark" (*Clayhanger*, 485). Throughout the trilogy
there are echoes of the theme. Hilda achieves a renascence
upon marrying Edwin, but her happiness is much dependent upon her retention of the vestiges of youth and
beauty.

In *Riceyman Steps* and elsewhere, even in the most
unlikely places, Bennett pursued his theme, with one of the
most dramatic portraits being in the late novel *Accident*,
where Mrs. Lucas is presented as a hag in whom Alan
detects faint reminders of the youth she must once have
known. She still has a bit of magnetism, but Alan sees the
end of her life as a tragedy: "her case crystallised and
illustrated the sorrowful curse of the human race: the
flight of time, of beauty, and of faculties" (88). Contrasting
Mrs. Lucas with the young Pearl, Bennett writes, "The
blonde face of the young beauty and the dark, seamed face
of the old hag . . . were very close together, and the contrast between them was at once dramatic and pathetic"
(226). Perhaps Bennett's memory once again reached back
to 1903 and the scene at the Duval, with the attractive
young waitress and the aging *maniaque*, from which, as we
have seen, grew his most intense study of a woman's
decline, that of Sophia Baines.

The evolution of gentle Constance from a girl to a
tottering old woman has pathetic overtones, but it was in
his depiction of the proud, rebellious, and handsome
Sophia that Bennett most relentlessly pursued his obsessive

theme. If Sophia had been docile, she would presumably have suffered no more than Constance. But she cannot accept fate unquestioningly, and so she is doomed to special suffering. Her very pride and her conscience increase the burden she must carry till life itself is exhausted. In lying about Gerald Scales and in neglecting her bedridden father Sophia has sinned, not only by Five-Towns standards, but by her own; and when she perceives the travesty of her marriage to the worthless Gerald, she is convinced of retribution: "In that moment she saw her acts with the terrible vision of a Hebrew prophet" (*The Old Wives' Tale*, 321). When Sophia's life is ended, Constance will sum it up from the same moral view. Her naïvely righteous judgment is not Bennett's, but significantly he indicates that it seems to fit: "It is strange how fate persists in justifying the harsh generalizations of Puritan morals . . . Sophia had sinned. It was therefore inevitable that she should suffer" (580).

Hardy had written in *Tess of the D'Urbervilles* of the human will to enjoy and the circumstantial will against enjoyment. Sophia has asserted the right to be happy. She has, however, made a fatal mistake, and the penalty does not depend on whether she has proceeded with sinful intent or only through immaturity. It stems entirely from her self-respect, and it is therefore severe: "She was one of those who are prepared to pay without grumbling for what they have had" (321). What she has had has been only a fleeting romance, and so the overpayment of continuing with Gerald until he deserts her and then enduring a lonely existence in Paris is incalculable. Bennett ironically credits Gerald with having completed Sophia's education: "He had not ruined her . . . because her moral force immeasurably exceeded his; he had unwittingly produced a masterpiece, but it was a tragic masterpiece" (346). Bennett reiterates her determination; she is now "ready to pay the price of pride and of a moment's im-becility with a lifetime of repression. It was high, but it was the price" (346).

The adventures which await Sophia as she struggles through the days of the Commune and wins modest prosperity in her highly respectable pension are as roman-tic as Bennett could create, but Sophia is aware of them only as tests of her Baines will. Pride and recovery of sound practical sense insure her from more folly and from hazard; but her days stretch on, devoid of gentleness and of love and with the certainty of ultimate defeat. Bennett stresses the change that has imperceptibly crept upon her. She is still handsome, but with a face "withered and crossed with lines." A stranger upon seeing her, or a woman like her, would be inclined to say, "When she was young she must have been worth looking at!"—with, Bennett adds, "a little transient regret that beautiful women cannot remain for ever young" (458). The hypothetical stranger may appear to be only a worldly sensualist, who sees women as a mere delectation of the eye. For the reader, however, who is not a stranger, his words are an understatement of the ravage that has taken place within.

When, worn and tired, Sophia returns to Bursley, she recalls her childhood as a beautiful time, but as for the long years that have intervened—"not for millions of pounds would she live her life over again" (502). The worst blow is still to come. By Puritan standards Gerald Scales deserves whatever punishment may befall a wastrel and irresponsible fool. But as Sophia looks at the dead man's hideous face, she feels only pity, born of her own experience: "Oh! how tired he must have been!" Her reflections are, of course, Bennett's own:

> Youth and vigour had come to that. Youth and vigour always came to that. Everything came to that. . . . She

saw him young, and proud, and strong . . . and now he
was old, and worn, and horrible, and dead. It was the
riddle of life that was puzzling and killing her. (572)

Bennett conveniently places a mirror in the room that
Sophia may glimpse a "tall, forlorn woman, who had
once been young and now was old." Until she looks on
Scales's corpse Sophia has been able to seem younger than
her sixty years, for strength of will has kept her straight
and tall; but when her death quickly follows the shock, the
truth comes cruelly forth: "with her twisted face, her
sightless orbs, her worn skin—she did not seem sixty, but
seventy! She was like something exhausted, and thrown
aside!" (581).

In the history of Sophia we have the antithesis of the
monologue by Browning's rabbi. Living has brought her
none of the wisdom that fills the meditations of a philosophic mind. Though she has been shown kindness and has
been desired by men, she has never had a true friend, and,
far from immersing herself in concern for the welfare of
her fellow men, she has remained aloof and lonely. Hence
it would be easy to agree with Constance, whose sadness
at her death is tinctured with a sense of retribution—
"God is not mocked!" (581). If one rejects such a moral
condemnation, prudence may replace a vengeful god; and
certainly prudence says that there was something most
unwise in Sophia's yielding first to adolescent impulse and
then to pride. And if prudence does not convince one,
then the very faith that keeps him going from day to day
cries out that there must be more to life than this.

Yet the claims of morality and prudence and faith may
be superficial and unjust. Bennett has never said that
Sophia is a mere personable hedonistic animal. Indeed, if
she were she would suffer less, for she could take each day
as it came; and when life seemed too hard to bear she
could turn to drink or make of the routine of existence

some kind of anodyne to blunt her awareness of the pain. Instead, she has endured the bitterness without a moment's flinch. And she has not had a mere negative existence, for she has always had an ideal concept of herself and of her role. Once she has recognized her initial mistake she has maintained an image of herself that even strangers can admire. Indeed, she *has* made of her life a masterpiece, the only kind she has known how to create. She has managed to stand utterly alone in a world she cannot begin to comprehend. If she has cried in anguish against destiny, she has done so in the privacy of her mind. And it has taken a succession of blows to beat her to her knees. When the nakedness of her soul is rudely exposed in death, fate has at last triumphed only because the will is now gone that could resist so shameful a rape.

A belief that one shared an affinity with another human spirit might, though not inevitably, turn life into a romance. If even for a brief moment one lacked such a belief he might feel lost in an unfamiliar universe. Sometimes, as in *Carlotta*, Bennett spells out such a sense of isolation. Discounting the rhetorical style of Carlotta's memoir, we may still feel the intensity of her despair alone and bewildered in Paris. She writes of the "horror of solitude in a vast city" and continues, "Oh, you solitary, you who have felt that horror descending upon you, desolating, clutching, and chilling the heart, you will comprehend me" (204–205). Sometimes, as with Lawrence Ridware, married to a cannibalistic woman, the loneliness is implied. For Elsie it is an oppression which she cannot describe and from which she can try to escape only by eating or drudgery.

The Pretty Lady, written in wartime, has overtones of man's inherent loneliness and at times even of the meaninglessness of social existence. Its hero, G. J. Hoape, is nearing fifty, the age when, Bennett chose to believe, life might offer the unexpected, and for Hoape it provides for a short while the illusion of romance. That illusion, however, is a tawdry thing, for in becoming the protector of Christine he understands her not at all, and she is hardly more than a worrisome possession. At the end, with no awareness that her yearning to contribute somehow to the war effort accounts for her unfaithfulness, he can only sever their shabby bond. A man with no useful work to do, he must bitterly dissipate his small talents in fatuous wartime busywork. Surrounded by women, he is an outsider in their world; he is drawn to them, yet is angered by the trivialities to which they subject him. There are, to be sure, glimpses of something better, but mainly the portrait is of a little man, sensual, but not evil, trying to live an orderly and rather decent life without knowing why. There are values which society cherishes, and so he, too, accepts them. There are ways of conducting one's affairs, including sexual gratifications, which would be messy, and he dislikes messiness; so with imperfect success he avoids it. But he is a lonely man. With no one can he discuss the things that most trouble him, and he cannot make the world reshape itself to his needs. Being treated like a monarch by a shop clerk or being treated like a sultan by Christine—these are only deceptive proofs of his importance. He is not really important at all, and importance itself is not what finally matters. He is just a very small man in a limitless universe, and—like Christine—he is alone.

Characters in Bennett may either accept the confinement of a narrow world, as Constance usually does, or, like Sophia, try to break free. When they attempt to desert their familiar universe, they find themselves in a realm of bewilderment or even terror and can only resort to the habits which they have renounced. A sense of futility overcomes them when they see life rapidly going to waste in spite of their efforts to salvage a little from the daily flow. Sooner or later both those who flee and those who remain become preoccupied with the small details that are measurable and have the appearance of being real. But even the ones, like Clayhanger, who do find some romance, have periods of frustration and ennui. At times they seem virtually in a nihilistic darkness with nothing outside themselves to serve as an ideal.

The Glimpse, like *Carlotta*, suffers from too heightened a style, but it is an honest effort to represent the wilderness into which man can stray before he is aware of where he has wandered. In one passage Loring relates his sensation of an ennui which was not new among writers in 1909, but was very personal for Bennett. Annoyed because a concert audience fails to enjoy a new form of music, that of Ravel, he continues:

> From such a common disappointment I had passed by swift, illogical stages, into an overwhelming sense of the universal absurd and mournful futility of things, a mood against which my faith in that beauty grimly battled in vain. The inadequacy of the cause proved only that my malady was gaining on me; perhaps it was gaining upon the world. And my malady was the celebrated malady of existence. (26)

In *The Regent* it is the card himself, Denry Machin, who at the outset apprehends the loss of romance and the settling in of an uneventful middle age. His wife's acceptance of a commonplace existence leaves him in spiritual isolation, and only through immersing himself in activities without questioning their value under the eye of eternity can he dispel his feeling of the arid banality of an apparently successful life.

When the character himself is weak, his frustration becomes destructive. Perhaps the best example is Fearns, of *Whom God Hath Joined*, who brings wretchedness to his wife and daughter and his mistress, not because he has begun with evil intent, but because philandering is an illusory escape from unhappiness and boredom. Usually, however, the characters are of average strength and courage, and they simply endure.

In the *Clayhanger* novels the high points of Edwin's pleasure are fewer than the stretches of bleakness and pain. Typical is his realization that his father's death has left him as unfree as before: "his existence would still be essentially the same—incomplete and sterile. He accepted the destiny, but he was daunted by it" (*Clayhanger*, 407). Even though he is later to feel that Hilda has made his life a romance, depression can still descend upon him, and he can ask himself, "what is the use of all these things— success, dignity, importance, luxury, love, sensuality, order, moral superiority? He foresaw thirty years of breakfasts, with plenty of the finest home-cured bacon and fresh eggs, but no romance" (*These Twain*, 140). His frustration is matched by Hilda's. Not a serious reader, and detesting such feminine pursuits as fancy work, social duties, and charitable functions, she sees herself having "descended into marriage as into a lotus valley. And more than half her life was gone" (350).

It is not inconsistent that such moods should be emphasized in a narrative that ends with the tone of romance. Bennett was not presenting them as mere depressions to be overcome. They are not transitory afflictions which will finally disappear. Quite the contrary, they will recur as certainly as they have returned in the past. The lives of Edwin and Hilda are too gray for them to cease.

At a time when much of the "sterile banality" of pension life still awaits her and before she has had to face unmistakably the advent of age, Sophia and Chirac are on a street in Paris. Sophia has been glad to have the sincere, but weak Chirac for an admirer, but his proposal that she become his mistress takes away the one illusion of affinity which she has ever known with another human being. As they go from a restaurant into the street, its dusky gloom accentuates Sophia's own. She is to have other shocks, but at the moment she is suffering a primordial sadness inherent in the very nature of men and women and love. Bennett writes:

> The gloom was awful; it was desolating. The universal silence seemed to be the silence of despair. Steeped in woe, Sophia thought wearily upon the hopeless problem of existence. For it seemed to her that she and Chirac had created this woe out of nothing, and yet it was an incurable woe! (*The Old Wives' Tale*, 426)

The "hopeless problem" is not to be solved by Sophia. The last book of *The Old Wives' Tale* bears the title "What Life Is." What it is includes some things that are amusing and cheerful; but it includes especially the deaths of two sisters and the decline of St. Luke's Square. Indeed, it ends with Fossette, Sophia's aged French poodle, tottering toward a soup plate, not because she loves food, but presumably because life must be endured until it runs down.

The hopelessness of the problem is implied in later novels, and it is significantly dealt with in the last major works, *Lord Raingo*, of 1926, and *The Imperial Palace*, of 1930. As Sam Raingo's mind wanders, he tries to review his life. He feels no guilt for the abyss that came to separate him from his wife, nor for having taken young Delphine as a mistress: "He was not to blame. Life was to blame, and he couldn't help that." His immediately following thoughts are not cynical; they merely represent futility: "He did not understand God and he did not understand life either, and he wasn't going to bother. He was tired and bored, and it was not his job to answer conundrums. A nice thing!" (*Lord Raingo*, 385). His declining to bother is

no answer. It permits him to drift to a pleasant vision of
Delphine, but it is when her image vanishes that he finds
himself "all alone again in the awful void."

Diverse elements make up *The Imperial Palace*, some of
them very light and entertaining. But Evelyn Orcham, the
hero, is given to ennui and melancholy. It is during one
of his periods of world weariness that Bennett paraphrases
his thoughts in words already cited: "Why are we anywhere? Why is anything? Is there after all a key to the
preposterous enigma of the universe?" As his adventure is
interrupted at the end of the novel he is no nearer to
unlocking the enigma. He has a wife now and is again
busy managing the luxury hotel. He is not sure whether
marriage or his work is the more important, or even
whether luxury hotels are "sociologically justifiable": "He
didn't know. He couldn't decide." What then is left for
him? Sophia has turned from the specter of "incurable
woe" to the dreary routine of her pension. As for Orcham:
"He knew merely that he was going straight on. He said
to himself: 'There's a lot of things in this world you'll
never get the hang of. And only idiots try to'" (769).

The words are reminiscent of Raingo's. Orcham can
return to his work, and he does have the good fortune to be
interested in managing for its own sake. But he is vulner-
able, for there is no noble mission to draw him out of
himself. When he retires at night he knows only that, more
or less successfully, he has met the daily problems that will
recur tomorrow and tomorrow, until he retires for good
and the hotel goes on as before, and patrons as indifferent
as Fossette toddle to their dinners and their beds.

The histories of the protagonists in *The Old Wives' Tale*,
Riceyman Steps, and *Lord Raingo* end with the solemnity of
tragedy. *Clayhanger* and *Hilda Lessways* conclude with a
recognition of the burden of existence. *These Twain* depicts
the resiliency of Edwin and Hilda, and ends with romance;

but it is a very sober romance that has been dearly bought. The tone at the end of *The Imperial Palace* is mixed. Orcham is pleased enough with Violet as his wife, but the grayness is all about him.

As we noted, there are incidents in *The Imperial Palace* that are reminiscent of *The Card* and melodramatic episodes that are almost fantasias. There are sentimental scenes involving head and heart that are Prohackian. And yet Bennett felt that in this huge book he was giving epic proportions to the life of a rather typical man engaged in one of the managerial careers fundamental to civilization. Evelyn Orcham and others like him are indispensable if men are to exist as social beings. In this respect the novel is realistic. There was no reason why it should achieve a tragic climax. Instead, it reflects the sensation of life of a man who has worked hard and who is bewildered. Like his creator, Orcham can perhaps conclude that his daily routine provides him "as near a regular happiness" as he can ever expect. Having accepted such a state of affairs, however, he remains in a slowly darkening autumnal world. If, having asked "Why are we anywhere?" he does not await a reply, it is not because Bennett considers the question of minor relevance. It is because he could only reject traditional answers.

It is, in short, a melancholy view with which Bennett has to end—a view which accepts the inherent absurdity of things. At the same time, it brings with it a sense of wonder—that men and women do bear up and live with decorum and personal dignity in a universe whose values they cannot comprehend. In a mild, usually quiet manner, they are very heroic indeed. Their lives, at once romantic and pathetic, are the best evidence Bennett could find of the "miraculous interestingness of the universe."

Chronology of Bennett's Works

The date given is of the first publication in book form. Cinema scenarios and journalistic articles not reprinted are not included.————

1898   *Journalism for Women: A Practical Guide*
        A Man from the North
1899   *Polite Farces for the Drawing Room*
1901   *Fame and Fiction: An Enquiry into Certain Popularities*
        (articles reprinted from the *Academy*)
1902   *Anna of the Five Towns: A Novel*
        The Grand Babylon Hotel
1903   *The Gates of Wrath: A Melodrama* (serialized October 1, 1899, ff.)
        How to Become an Author
        Leonora: A Novel
        The Truth about an Author (reprinted from the *Academy*)
1904   *A Great Man*
        Teresa of Watling Street
1905   *The Loot of Cities: Being the Adventures of a Millionaire in Search of Joy (a Fantasia) and Other Stories*

Sacred and Profane Love (revised and republished in
1911 as *The Book of Carlotta*)

Tales of the Five Towns (including some stories
written much earlier)

1906 *Hugo: A Fantasia on Modern Times*

The Sinews of War (with Eden Phillpots)

Things That Interested Me, First Series (privately
printed)

Whom God Hath Joined

1907 *The City of Pleasure: A Fantastic Phantasia*

The Ghost: A Modern Fantasy (first serialized as *For
Love and Life*)

The Grim Smile of the Five Towns

The Reasonable Life (republished as *Mental Efficiency
and Other Hints to Men and Women*. Reprinted from
T. P.'s Weekly)

*Things Which Have Interested Me: Being Leaves from a
Journal Kept by Arnold Bennett, Second Series*
(privately printed)

1908 *Buried Alive*

Cupid and Commonsense (a play based on *Anna of the
Five Towns*)

How to Live on Twenty-Four Hours a Day (reprinted
from the *Evening News*)

The Old Wives' Tale

The Statue (with Eden Phillpots)

Things Which Have Interested Me, Third Series
(privately printed)

1909 *The Glimpse: An Adventure of the Soul*

The Human Machine (reprinted from *T. P.'s Weekly*)

*Literary Taste: How to Form It, with Detailed Instruc-
tions for Collecting a Complete Library of English
Literature*

What the Public Wants: A Play in Four Acts

1910 *Clayhanger*

Florentine Journal

Helen with the High Hand

1911   *The Card: A Story of the Five Towns* (reprinted as *Denry the Audacious*)

The Feast of St. Friend (reprinted as *Friendship and Happiness*)

Hilda Lessways

The Honeymoon: A Comedy in Three Acts

1912   *The Matador of the Five Towns*

Milestones: A Play in Three Acts (with Edward Knoblock)

Your United States: Impressions of a First Visit (published in England as *Those United States*)

1913   *The Great Adventure: A Play in Four Acts* (based on *Buried Alive*)

Paris Nights and Other Impressions of Places and People

The Plain Man and His Wife

The Regent: A Five-Towns Story of Adventure in London

1914   *The Author's Craft*

From the Log of the Velsa

Liberty: A Statement of the British Case

The Price of Love

1915   *Over There: War Scenes on the Western Front*

1916   *The Lion's Share*

These Twain

1917   *Books and Persons: Being Comments on a Past Epoch 1908–1911* (articles reprinted from the *New Age*)

1918   *The Pretty Lady*

The Roll Call

Self and Self-Management: Essays about Existing

The Title: A Comedy in Three Acts

1919   *Judith: A Play in Three Acts Founded on the Apocryphal Book of "Judith"*

Sacred and Profane Love: A Play in Four Acts Founded upon the Novel of the Same Name

1920   *Our Women: Chapters on the Sex-Discord*
1921   *Things That Have Interested Me*
1922   *Body and Soul: A Play in Four Acts*
       Lilian
       The Love Match: A Play in Five Scenes
       Mr. Prohack
1923   *Don Juan de Marana: A Play in Four Acts*
       How to Make the Best of Life
       Riceyman Steps
       Things That Have Interested Me (Second Series)
1924   *Elsie and the Child*
       London Life: A Play in Three Acts and Nine Scenes
          (with Edward Knoblock)
1926   *The Bright Island* (written in 1920)
       Lord Raingo
       Things That Have Interested Me: Third Series
1927   *Mr. Prohack: A Comedy in Three Acts* (with Edward
          Knoblock)
       The Vanguard (published in England as *The Strange
          Vanguard: A Fantasia*)
       The Woman Who Stole Everything (reprints of stories)
1928   *Mediterranean Scenes: Rome-Greece-Constantinople*
       The Savour of Life: Essays in Gusto (reprints of articles)
1929   *Accident*
       My Religion (by Bennett and others, n.d.)
       The Religious Interregnum (booklet)
1930   *The Imperial Palace*
       Journal 1929
1931   *The Night Visitor and Other Stories* (reprints)
1932   *Dream of Destiny, an Unfinished Novel, and Venus
          Rising from the Sea* (the latter published in
          America as *Stroke of Luck*)
1933   *Flora* (acted in 1927)
       The Journal of Arnold Bennett (edited by Newman
          Flower)

Bibliography

BENNETT'S CRITICAL WRITINGS

The Author's Craft and Other Critical Writings of Arnold Bennett. Edited by Samuel Hynes. Lincoln: University of Nebraska Press, 1968.

EDITIONS OF BENNETT LETTERS

(In chronological order)

Bennett, Dorothy Cheston. *Arnold Bennett: A Portrait Done at Home, Together with 170 Letters from Arnold Bennett.* New York: Kendall and Sharp, 1935.

Arnold Bennett's Letters to His Nephew. Edited by Richard Bennett, with a preface by Frank Swinnerton. New York: Harper and Brothers, 1935.

Arnold Bennett and H. G. Wells: A Record of a Personal and Literary Friendship. Edited by Harris Wilson. Urbana: University of Illinois Press, 1960.

Correspondance André Gide-Arnold Bennett: Vingt Ans d'Amitié Litteraire (1911–1931). Geneva: Librairie Droz, 1964.

Letters of Arnold Bennett. Edited by James Hepburn. Vol. I: *Letters to J. B. Pinker.* London: Oxford University Press, 1966. Vol. II: *Letters 1889–1915.* London: Oxford University Press, 1968. Vol. III: *Letters 1916–1931.* London: Oxford University Press, 1970.

SELECTED STUDIES OF BENNETT
(In chronological order)

James, Henry. *Notes on Novelists, with Some Other Notes.* New York: Charles Scribner's Sons, 1914.

Darton, F. J. Harvey. *Arnold Bennett.* New York: Henry Holt, 1915.

Hughes, Dorothea P. "The Novels of Mr. Arnold Bennett and Wesleyan Methodism," *The Contemporary Review,* CX (1916), 602–610.

Scott, Dixon. *Men of Letters.* New York: Hodder and Stoughton, 1917. (The chapter on Bennett—"The Commonsense of Mr. Arnold Bennett"—is reprinted from the *Manchester Guardian,* 1911–1913.)

Sherman, Stuart Pratt. *On Contemporary Literature.* New York: Henry Holt, 1917. (The chapter "The Realism of Arnold Bennett" is reprinted from the *Nation.*)

Follett, Helen T. and Wilson. *Some Modern Novelists: Appreciations and Estimates.* New York: Henry Holt, 1919. Pp. 206–232.

Goldring, Douglas. *Reputations: Essays in Criticism.* New York: Thomas Seltzer, 1920. ("The Gordon Selfridge of English Letters," pp. 147–156.)

Priestley, J. B. *Figures in Modern Literature.* London: John Lane, 1924. Pp. 3–30.

Bennett, Marguerite. *Arnold Bennett.* London: A. M. Philpot, 1925.

Drew, Elizabeth A. *The Modern Novel: Some Aspects of Contemporary Fiction.* New York: Harcourt, Brace and Company, 1926. Pp. 199–219.

West, Rebecca. *The Strange Necessity: Essays and Reviews.* London: Jonathan Cape, 1928. Pp. 199–213.

Cross, Wilbur. "Arnold Bennett of the Five Towns," *The Yale Review,* New Series, XVIII (1929), 302–319.

Byrne, M. S. "Arnold Bennett and His Critics," *The National Review,* XCVI (1931), 702–706.

Maugham, W. Somerset. "Arnold Bennett," *Life and Letters*, VI (1931), 413–422.

West, Rebecca. *Arnold Bennett Himself*. The John Day Pamphlets, 1931.

Bennett, Marguerite. *My Arnold Bennett*. New York: Dutton and Company, 1932.

Scott-James, R. A. *Personality in Literature: 1913–1931*. New York: Henry Holt, 1932. Pp. 77–95.

West, Geoffrey [Wells, Geoffrey H.]. *The Problem of Arnold Bennett*. London: Johnson and Steele, 1932.

Smith, Pauline. *A.B. ". . . a Minor Marginal Note."* London: Jonathan Cape, 1933.

Wells, H. G. *Experiment in Autobiography*. New York: Macmillan, 1934. Pp. 523–540 and *passim*.

Wheatley, Elizabeth D. "Arnold Bennett's Trifles: His Novels for the Gay Middle-Aged," *The Sewanee Review*, XLII (1934), 180–189.

Simons, J. B. *Arnold Bennett and His Novels: A Critical Study*. Oxford: Basil Blackwell, 1936.

Lafourcade, Georges. *Arnold Bennett: A Study*. London: Frederick Miller, 1939.

Locherbie-Goff, Margaret. *La Jeunesse d'Arnold Bennett (1867–1904)*. Avesnes-sur Helpe: Editions de "L'Observateur," 1939.

Wagenknecht, Edward. *Cavalcade of the English Novel*. New York: Henry Holt and Company, 1954 (copyright, 1943).

Atkins, J. B. *Incidents and Reflections*. London: Christophers, 1947. Pp. 174–182.

Prichett, V. S. *The Living Novel*. New York: Reynal and Hitchcock, 1947. ("The Five Towns," pp. 130–135.)

Allen, Walter. *Arnold Bennett*. London: Home and Van Thal, 1948.

Conacher, W. M. "Arnold Bennett and the French Realists," *Queen's Quarterly*, LVI, No. 3 (1949), 400–417.

Flower, Newman. *Just as It Happened*. London: Cassell, 1950. Pp. 157–168.

Swinnerton, Frank. *Arnold Bennett*. London: Longmans, Green and Company, 1950.

Pound, Reginald. *Arnold Bennett: A Biography*. New York: Harcourt, Brace and Company, 1953.

Sanna, Vittoria. *Arnold Bennett e i Romanzi delle Cinque Città*. Florence: Marzocco, 1953.

Hepburn, James G. "Arnold Bennett Manuscripts and Rare Books: A List of Holdings," *English Fiction in Transition*, II, No. 2 (1958), 23–29.

Hall, James. *Arnold Bennett: Primitivism and Taste*. Seattle: University of Washington Press, 1959.

Hepburn, James G. "The Two Worlds of Edwin Clayhanger," *Boston University Studies in English*, V, No. 4 (1961), 246–255.

———. "Manuscript Notes for *Lord Raingo*," *English Fiction in Transition*, V, No. 1 (1962), 1–5.

———. "Some Curious Realism in *Riceyman Steps*," *Modern Fiction Studies*, VIII, No. 2 (1962), 116–126.

Kreuz, Irving. "Mr. Bennett and Mrs. Woolf," *Modern Fiction Studies*, VIII, No. 2 (1962), 103–115.

Hepburn, James G. *The Art of Arnold Bennett*. Bloomington: Indiana University Press, 1963.

———. "The Notebook for *Riceyman Steps*," *PMLA*, LXXVIII, No. 3 (1963), 257–261.

Kennedy, James G. "Reassuring Facts in *The Pretty Lady*, *Lord Raingo*, and Modern Novels," *English Literature in Transition*, VII, No. 3 (1964), 131–142.

Barker, Dudley. *Writer by Trade: A Portrait of Arnold Bennett*. New York: Atheneum, 1966.

Tillier, Louis. *Arnold Bennett et ses romans réalistes*. Paris: Didier, 1967.

Index